ALSO BY MARK R. LEVIN

*Plunder and Deceit*

*The Liberty Amendments*

*Ameritopia*

*Liberty and Tyranny*

*Rescuing Sprite*

*Men in Black*

# REDISCOVERING AMERICANISM

## AND THE TYRANNY OF PROGRESSIVISM

Mark R. Levin

THRESHOLD EDITIONS

New York London Toronto Sydney New Delhi

Threshold Editions
An Imprint of Simon & Schuster, Inc.
1230 Avenue of the Americas
New York, NY 10020



First Threshold Editions hardcover edition July 2017

THRESHOLD EDITIONS and colophon are trademarks of Simon & Schuster, Inc.

For information about special discounts for bulk purchases, please contact Simon & Schuster Special Sales at 1-866-506-1949 or business@simonandschuster.com.

The Simon & Schuster Speakers Bureau can bring authors to your live event. For more information, or to book an event, contact the Simon & Schuster Speakers Bureau at 1-866-248-3049 or visit our website at www.simonspeakers.com.

Interior design by Davina Mock

Manufactured in the United States of America

10 9 8 7 6 5 4 3 2 1

Library of Congress Cataloging-in-Publication Data is available.

ISBN 978-1-4767-7308-7
ISBN 978-1-4767-7347-6 (ebook)

*To my wonderful parents,*
*Jack and Norma*

# CONTENTS

ONE

# AMERICANISM

I OFTEN WONDER WHAT Thomas Jefferson, George Washington, James Madison, John Adams, George Mason, Benjamin Franklin, and the other Founders would think about today's America. What about the earliest Boston revolutionaries, men like Samuel Adams, Joseph Warren, John Hancock, and Paul Revere? Of course, they would be mesmerized by all the modern inventions and conveniences of everyday life, but what of the ubiquitous nature of the federal government? Surely they would object.

In *Liberty and Tyranny* I wrote: "So distant is America today from its founding principles that it is difficult to precisely describe the nature of American government. It is not strictly a constitutional republic, because the Constitution has been and continues to be easily altered by a judicial oligarchy that mostly enforces, if not expands, the Statist's agenda. It is not strictly a representative republic, because so many edicts are produced by a maze of administrative departments that are unknown to the public and detached from its sentiment. It is not strictly a federal republic, because the states that gave the central government life now live at its behest. What, then, is it? It is a society steadily transitioning toward statism."[1]

Moreover, do most Americans appreciate liberty, the civil society, republicanism, and economic prosperity or fear their loss? Of course, if you ask someone the question about himself, he is likely to answer yes, although he might wonder about his fellow citizens' grasp and gratitude. But the issue is more perplexing and vital to the future of the American republic than one might initially imagine. An incalculable number of philosophers and scholars, ancient to modern, have written extensively about these topics. It is beyond my mortal competence or the physical limitations of this book to catalog or probe them all here. Although five of my six earlier books have addressed these subjects in various ways, there is great value if not urgency in exploring them further from an additional or a more thorough perspective, given what I believe to be their precariousness in modern America. Thus we must tackle the matter of first principles. After all, this is our heritage. This is not a mere academic or theoretical exercise among elitists, of interest only to professors and navel-gazers. It sits at the core of human existence and American society and, therefore, is relevant to us all. These principles, and understanding them, serve as the antidote to tyrannical regimes and governments.

I am well aware that this book will not change the course of history. But if it can open a few eyes it will have served its purpose. I shall do my best to make my writing accessible and interesting to the broadest audience without compromising content. In this book, I quote substantially and directly from various philosophers and thinkers to provide the reader with a real understanding and feel for what is being argued and proposed. In addition to extensive endnotes, I also provide book and essay titles and sources throughout the body of this book, thereby making it easier for the reader to go to those sources on their own should they want to further explore them. Nonetheless, this book will require the reader's focus and engagement as it covers much material in relatively short order.

---

It is fitting to begin our journey with the final letter written by one of America's greatest Founders, Thomas Jefferson. On June 24, 1826, Jefferson, who was quite ill, wrote to Roger Weightman from Monticello, declining his invitation to participate in the fiftieth-anniversary celebration of the Declaration of Independence. Jefferson would become bedridden two days later and die on July 4, the same day his good friend in later years, John Adams, passed away.

In great pain from numerous ailments, and now writing

with his left hand since he had earlier broken his right hand, which never healed properly, Jefferson wrote:

Monticello
June 24. 1826

Respected Sir

The kind invitation I receive from you on the part of the citizens of the city of Washington, to be present with them at their celebration of the 50th. anniversary of American independence; as one of the surviving signers of an instrument pregnant with our own, and the fate of the world, is most flattering to myself, and heightened by the honorable accompaniment proposed for the comfort of such a journey. [I]t adds sensibly to the sufferings of sickness, to be deprived by it of a personal participation in the rejoicings of that day. [B]ut acquiescence is a duty, under circumstances not placed among those we are permitted to control. *I should, indeed, with peculiar delight, have met and exchanged there congratulations personally with the small band, the remnant of that host of worthies, who joined with us on that day, in the bold and doubtful election we were to make for our country, between submission or the sword; and to have enjoyed with them the consolatory fact, that our fellow citizens, after half a century of experience and prosperity, continue to approve the choice we made.* [M]*ay it be to the world, what I believe it will be, (to some parts sooner, to others later, but finally to all,) the Signal of arousing men to burst the chains, under which monkish ignorance and superstition had persuaded them to bind themselves, and to assume the blessings & security of self-government.* [T]*hat form which we have substituted, restores the free right to the unbounded exercise of reason and freedom of opinion.* [A]*ll eyes are opened, or opening, to the rights of man.* [T]*he general spread of the light of science has already laid open to every view.* [T]*he palpable truth, that the mass of mankind has not been born with saddles on their backs, nor a favored few booted and spurred, ready to ride them legitimately, by the grace of God.* [T]*hese are grounds of hope for others.* [F]*or ourselves, let the annual return of this day forever refresh our recollections of these rights, and an undiminished devotion to them.* (Italics added)

I will ask permission here to express the pleasure with which I should have met my ancient neighbors of the City of Washington and of its vicinities, with whom I passed so many years of a pleasing social intercourse; an intercourse which so much relieved the anxieties of the public cares, and left impressions so deeply engraved in my affections, as never to be forgotten. With my regret that ill health forbids me the gratification of an acceptance, be pleased to receive for yourself, and those for whom you write, the assurance of my highest respect and friendly attachments.

Th. Jefferson[2]

As Jefferson wished, we now "refresh our recollection of these rights" and turn straightaway to the Declaration of Independence and carefully examine its language. Its wording is crucial and purposeful. And its link to *natural law* is inextricable and imperative. It begins as follows: "When in the Course of human events, it becomes necessary for one people to dissolve the political bands which have connected them with another, and to assume among the powers of the earth, the separate and equal station to which the *Laws of Nature* and of *Nature's God* entitle them, a decent respect to the opinions of mankind." It states further: "We hold these truths to be *self-evident*, that *all men are created equal*, that they are *endowed by their Creator with certain unalienable Rights*, that among these are *Life*, *Liberty and the pursuit of Happiness*."[3] (Italics added)

The near-universal appeal of this wording and these principles among America's Founders is underscored further in other important historical documents of this period. The Virginia Declaration of Rights was adopted on June 12, 1776, thereby predating the Declaration of Independence by a few weeks. It was principally drafted by George Mason, who would also play a significant role at the Constitutional Convention in 1787. The prominence of the Virginia Declaration is indisputable as some of its language was, in fact, borrowed by Jefferson in drafting the Declaration of Independence. Moreover, Benjamin Franklin, John Adams, and Samuel Adams used similar language in drafting future declarations of rights and constitutions for their own states.

Section 1 of the Virginia Declaration provides: "That *all men are by nature equally free and independent* and *have certain inherent rights*, of which, when they enter into a state of society, they cannot, by any compact, deprive or divest their posterity; namely, *the enjoyment of life and liberty*, with the means of *acquiring and possessing property*, and *pursuing and obtaining happiness and safety*."[4] (Italics added)

The Pennsylvania Declaration of Rights, adopted on August 16, 1776, and whose main author was Franklin, states, in Section 1: "That *all men are born equally free and independent*, and *have certain natural, inherent and inalienable rights*, amongst which are, the *enjoying and defending life and liberty, acquiring, possessing and protecting property*, and *pursuing and obtaining happiness and safety*."[5] (Italics added)

Article I of the Massachusetts Declaration of Rights, adopted in 1780, and whose authors included John Adams and Samuel Adams, states: "All *men are born free and equal*, and *have certain natural, essential, and unalienable rights*; among which may be reckoned the right of *enjoying and defending their lives and liberties*; that of *acquiring, possessing, and protecting property*; in fine, that of seeking *and obtaining their safety and happiness*."[6] (Italics added)

But the Declaration of Independence rightly stands as the formal, consensus proclamation for America's independence and founding. After several iterations, it was adopted by the Second Continental Congress, which had initially convened in Philadelphia in May 1775 after the battles of Lexington and

Concord. All the colonies were represented. And while most of the delegates initially opposed independence, as Congress's entreaties for peace were met with intensified British military aggression it became clear that the colonies would have to choose either independence or subjugation.

On May 8, 1825, forty-nine years after the adoption of the Declaration of Independence, in a letter replying to Henry Lee about the source of the ideas and language in the Declaration, Jefferson succinctly explained: "[W]ith respect to our rights, and the acts of the British government contravening those rights, there was but one opinion on this side of the water. All American whigs thought alike on these subjects. When forced, therefore, to resort to arms for redress, an appeal to the tribunal of the world was deemed proper for our justification. This was the object of the Declaration of Independence. Not to find out new principles, or new arguments, never before thought of, not merely to say things which had never been said before; but to place before mankind the common sense of the subject, in terms so plain and firm as to command their assent, and to justify ourselves in the independent stand we are compelled to take. Neither aiming at originality of principle or sentiment, nor yet copied from any particular and previous writing, it was intended to be *an expression of the American mind*, and to give to that expression the proper tone and spirit called for by the occasion. All its authority rests then *on the harmonizing sentiments of the day, whether expressed in conversation, in letters, printed essays, or in the elementary books of pub-*

*lic right, as Aristotle, Cicero, Locke, Sidney, &c*. The historical documents which you mention as in your possession, ought all to be found, and I am persuaded you will find, to be corroborative of the facts and principles advanced in that Declaration."[7] (Italics added)

From where do these all-important ideas come? If we wish to truly understand liberty, the civil society, and America's founding—that is, our birthright—we must examine further, although in short, the philosophers Jefferson rightly cites as authorities upon whom he and the nation's forefathers relied for their illumination of *natural law*—which is the foundational principle at the core of American society. As will become apparent, philosophy and practical politics are linked and, therefore, have a real effect on the life of the individual.

The most influential philosopher during the revolutionary period was the indispensable English thinker John Locke (1632–1704), who in *The Second Treatise of Government* (1689) inspired countless leading American colonists and Founders, including the delegates who gathered at the Second Continental Congress. Indeed, having studied the philosophical origins of the American Revolution, Harvard University professor Bernard Bailyn found that "[i]n pamphlet after pamphlet the American writers cited Locke on natural rights and on the social and governmental contract. . . ."[8]

Locke wrote that man is born with God-given inalienable rights—among them, personal and individual liberty. "The state of Nature has a law of Nature to govern it, which obliges everyone, and reason, which is that law, teaches all mankind who will but consult it, that being all equal and independent, no one ought to harm another in life, health, liberty or possessions; for men being all the workmanship of one omnipotent and infinitely wise Maker; all the servants of one sovereign Master, sent into the world by His order and about his business; they are His property, whose workmanship they are made to last during His, not one another's pleasure. And being furnished with like faculties, sharing all in one community of Nature, there cannot be supposed any such subordination among us that may authorize us to destroy one another, as if we were made for one another's uses, as the inferior ranks of creatures are for ours. Everyone as he is bound to preserve himself, and not to quit his station willfully, so by the like reason, when his own preservation comes not in competition, ought to be as much as he can preserve the rest of mankind, and not unless it be to do justice on an offender, take away or impair the life or what tends to the preservation of life, the liberty, health, limb, or goods of another."[9]

Locke said that there is a circle of freedom surrounding each person and all people at birth. And within that circle is the absolute human right to live and live freely. This is a natural right born of natural law or the law of nature. It is divine and eternal, unalterable by mankind. Moreover, man also has the ability to reason. And it is through reason that he discovers and discerns natural law, his natural rights, and their application to all of humanity.

Let us explore further Locke's understanding of reason in this regard. In his essay "Is There a Rule of Morals, or Law of Nature Given to Us? Yes," Locke acknowledged that "there is the title of right reason, to which everyone who considers himself a human being lays claim, and that it is about which the various parties of men contend so fiercely among themselves, and which each one alleges to be the foundation of its doctrine. By reason, however, I do not think is meant here that faculty of the understanding which forms the trains of thought and deduces proofs, but certain definite principles of action from which springs all virtues and whatever is necessary for the proper moulding of morals. For that which is correctly derived from these principles is justly said to be in accordance with right reason."[10]

Locke explained further that while "all people are by nature endowed with reason, and I say that natural law can be known by reason, but from this it does not necessarily follow that it is known to any and every one. For there are some who make no use of the light of reason but prefer darkness and would not wish to show themselves to themselves. But even the sun shows a man the way to go, unless he opens his eyes and is well prepared for the journey. . . ."[11] In other words, the fact that every person has the ability to reason and discover natural law, and the divine rights that flow from it, does not mean that all people will do so.

In addition, Locke pointed out that natural law, not man-made law, is the origin and compass of human morality.

"[W]ithout natural law there would be neither virtue nor vice, neither the reward of goodness nor the punishment of evil: there is no fault, no guilt, where there is no law. Everything would have to depend on human will, and, since there would be nothing to demand dutiful action, it seems that man would not be bound to do anything but what utility or pleasure might recommend, or what a blind and lawless impulse might happen perchance to fasten on. The terms 'upright' and 'virtuous' would disappear as meaningless or be nothing at all but empty names. . . . [F]or the nature of good and evil is eternal and certain, and their value cannot be determined either by the public ordinances of men or by any private opinion."[12]

Even before Locke, the Greek philosopher Aristotle, the Roman philosopher Marcus Tullius Cicero, and the Italian philosopher Thomas Aquinas, among others, all explored the true nature of man and the meaning of his existence. Why does this matter? Again, it is the *foundation* of human morality on which republics are built, including and especially the American republic. The principle of natural law permeated American thought from the beginning of our republic and well before.

Aristotle (384–322 BC), a student of Plato, is one of mankind's greatest intellectuals and philosophers. Although not the first to do so, Aristotle identified the existence of natural law and, crucially, distinguished it from man-made law. Locke himself referred to Aristotle's "*Nicomachean Ethics* (350 BC), Book I, Chapter 7," pointing out that Aristotle "says that 'the special function of man is active exercise of the mind's faculties in accordance with rational principle.' For since in the preceding passages he had shown by various examples that there is a special sort of work each thing is designed to perform, he tried to find out what this may be in the case of a human being also. Thus, having taken account of all the operations of the vegetal and sentient faculties which men have in common with animals and plants, in the end he rightly concluded that the proper function of man is acting in conformity with reason, so much so that man must of necessity perform what reason prescribes. Likewise in Book V, chapter 7, where he drew the distinction between legal justice and natural justice, Aristotle said 'A natural rule of justice is one which has the same validity everywhere.' Hence it is rightly concluded that there is a law of nature, since there is a law which obtains everywhere."[13]

Locke said that like Aristotle, man is different from other forms of life because, among other things, he has the unique ability to reason. As such, men can discover natural law and distinguish it from man-made law—between that which is naturally just and legally just. Indeed, the late scholar and philosopher Shirley Robin Letwin, author of *On the History of the Idea of Law* (2005), observed that Aristotle described "the twofold character of law . . . which he calls 'particular' and 'universal.' Particular law 'is that which each community lays down and applies to its own members'; universal law 'is the law of nature.' Because 'everyone to some extent divines' this 'law of nature,' we can know that it 'really is.' And because of this divine element in human nature, there is a 'natural justice and injustice common to all, even to those who have no association or covenant with each other.'"[14]

Why is this important? Remember the key language from the Declaration of Independence about "the Laws of Nature and of Nature's God"—divine and eternal law as distinguished from the rule of man, or in the Founders' case, the rule of one man—a monarch.

Let us break down the Declaration's terminology further. "We hold these truths to be self-evident" (knowable through right reason), "that all men are created equal, that they are endowed by their Creator with certain unalienable Rights" (the divine law of nature obtains everywhere and applies to all), "that among these are Life, Liberty and the pursuit of Happiness" (the right to live freely and happily).

Also referenced in Jefferson's letter is Cicero (106–43 BC), an iconic Roman scholar, philosopher, and statesman. As Cicero explained, justice—that is, truth and virtue—is intrinsic to the state of nature: "If the principles of Justice were founded on the decrees of peoples, the edicts of princes, or the decisions of judges, then Justice would sanction robbery and adultery and forgery of wills, in case these acts were approved by the votes or decrees of the populace. But if so great a power belongs to the decisions and decrees of fools that the laws of Nature can be changed by their votes, then why do they not ordain that what is bad and baneful shall be considered good and salutary? Or, if a law can make Justice out of Injustice, can it not also make good out of bad? But in fact we can perceive the difference between good laws and bad by referring them to no other standard than Nature: indeed, it is not merely Justice and Injustice which are distinguished by Nature, but also and without exception things which are honorable and dishonorable. For since an intelligence common to us all makes things known to us and formulates them in our minds, honorable actions are ascribed by us to virtue, and dishonorable actions are matters of opinion, and not fixed by Nature."[15]

Therefore, Cicero argues that the source of justice, truth, virtue, etc.—in a word, morality—is natural law. It is permanent and supreme, unalterable by man or his institutions. Cicero wrote: "True law is *right reason* in agreement with nature; it is of universal application, unchanging and everlasting; it summons to duty by its commands, and averts from wrongdoing by its prohibitions. . . . It is a sin to try to alter this law, nor is it allowable to repeal any part of it, and it is impossible to abolish it entirely. We cannot be freed from its obligations by senate or people, and we need not look outside ourselves for an expounder or interpreter of it. And there will not be different laws at Rome and at Athens, or different laws now and in the future, but one eternal and unchangeable law will be valid for all nations and at all times, and there will be one master and ruler, that is God, over us all, for he is the author of this law, its promulgator and its enforcing judge. Whoever is disobedient is fleeing from himself and denying his human nature, and by reason of this very fact he will suffer the worst punishment."[16]

For contemporary readers, no doubt the least-known philosopher among those mentioned by Jefferson is Algernon Sidney (1623–1683). However, to Jefferson, John Adams, and numerous others during the American Revolutionary period, Sidney's treatise, *Discourses Concerning Government* (1680), was an essential work for which Sidney, among other reasons, was executed by King Charles II. Sidney wrote *Discourses* as a response to the proposition that the absolute rule of monarchs is by divine right.[17] A contemporary of Locke, Sidney wrote: "The common Notions of Liberty are not from School Divines, but from Nature. . . ." He added: "Tis hard to comprehend how one man can come to be master of many, equal to himself in right, unless it be by consent or by force. . . . No right can come by conquest, unless there were a right of making that conquest. . . ." In the end, he explained, "[t]o depend upon the Will of a Man is Slavery."[18]

Like others before him, Sidney believed that man uncovers the state of nature and natural law through reason. "Man's natural love to Liberty is temper'd by Reason, which originally is his Nature." "The truth is, man is hereunto led by reason which is his nature. Everyone sees they cannot well live asunder, nor many together, without some rule to which all must submit. This submission is a restraint of liberty, but could be of no effect as to the good intended, unless it were general; nor general, unless it were natural."[19]

It is important to emphasize that natural law provides a

moral compass or order—justice, virtue, truth, prudence, etc.—a fundamental, universal, everlasting harmony of mores that transcend human law. Through natural law discovered by right reason, man knows right from wrong and good from bad. Moreover, that which is naturally just may not be legally just. Again, we turn to Locke, given his stature during the American founding. He wrote that "without showing a law that commands or forbids [. . .], moral goodness will be but an empty sound, and those actions which the schools here call virtues or vices, may by the same authority be called by contrary names in another country; and if these be nothing more than their decisions and determinations in the case, they will be still nevertheless indifferent as to any man's practice, which will by such kind of determinations be under no obligation to observe them."[20]

Locke said, as have others, that natural law is forever and enduring, and man-made law, which may vary from place to place and time to time, clearly is not. That which is just and virtuous is just and virtuous regardless of the passage of laws or time. Indeed, as Cicero explained earlier, even just man-made laws and just republics are just because they spring from the principle of or reflect the essence of natural law. Natural law is superior to, and precedes, political and governmental institutions. For example, the Golden Rule—"Do unto others as you would have them do unto you"—is a universally recognized moral ethic. It is *the* Golden Rule because it is true and just.

Again, and importantly, this was the view of practically all of America's Founders. For example, in February 1775, Alexander Hamilton, later Jefferson's rival and frequent nemesis, wrote a lengthy and significant pamphlet, which was turned into a newspaper essay—*The Farmer Refuted, &c*—excoriating a particularly nasty objector to the growing American rebellion against the British Crown. Among other things, Hamilton stressed the natural rights of the individual: "Upon this [natural] law, depend the natural rights of mankind, the supreme being gave existence to man, together with the means of preserving and beatifying that existence. He endowed him with rational faculties, by the help of which, to discern and pursue such things, as were consistent with his duty and interest, and invested him with an inviolable right to personal liberty, and personal safety. Hence, in a state of nature, no man had any *moral* power to deprive another of his life, limbs, property or liberty; nor the least authority to command, or exact obedience from him; except that which arose from the ties of consanguinity. Hence also, the origin of all civil government, justly established, must be a voluntary compact, between the rulers and the ruled; and must be liable to such limitations, as are necessary for the security of the *absolute rights* of the latter; for what original title can any man or set of men have, to govern others, except their own consent? To usurp dominion over a people, in their own despite, or to grasp at a more extensive power than they are willing to entrust, is to violate that law of nature, which gives every man a right to his personal liberty; and can, therefore, confer no obligation to obedience."[21]

Throughout the discussion of natural law, there are obviously repeated references by philosophers, thinkers, and the Founders to God, divine providence, an eternal norm, etc. Turning again to the language of the Declaration of Independence, it states, in part, that all men are "*endowed by their Creator with certain unalienable rights . . .*" There is an appeal to "*the Supreme Judge of the world*" and "*a firm reliance on the protection of Divine Providence*."[22]

In *Liberty and Tyranny*, I ask and answer the question that is also relevant here: "Is it possible that there is no Natural Law and man can know moral and unalienable rights from his own reasoning, unaided by the supernatural or God? There are, of course, those who argue this case—including the Atheist and others who attempt to distinguish Natural Law from Divine Providence. It is not the view adopted by the Founders. This position would, it seems, lead man to arbitrarily create his own morality and rights, or create his own arbitrary morality and rights—right and wrong, just and unjust, good and bad, would be relative concepts susceptible to circumstantial applications. Moreover, by what justification would "Life, Liberty, and the pursuit of Happiness" be "unalienable Rights" if there is no Natural Law, since reason alone cannot make them inviolable? What then is Natural Law if its origin is unknown or rejected? It is nothing more than a human construct. An individual may benefit from the moral order and unalienable rights around which society functions while rejecting their Divine origin. But the civil society cannot organize itself that way. It would become unstable and vulnerable to anarchy and tyranny, imperiling all within it, especially the individual. The abandonment of Natural Law is the adoption of tyranny in one form or another, because there is no humane or benevolent alternative to Natural Law."[23]

"Some resist the idea of Natural Law's relationship to Divine Providence, for they fear it leads to intolerance or even theocracy. They have that backwards. If man is 'endowed by the Creator with certain unalienable rights,' he is endowed with these rights no matter his religion or whether he has allegiance to any religion."[24] Nonetheless, although America has deep religious roots, and the Founders were overwhelming religious men—albeit of varying religious intensity and Christian denominations—the Declaration of Independence and most of the arguments undergirding it were not per se expositions or assertions of a particular theological fidelity.

Many decades after America's founding, Abraham Lincoln relied heavily on the Declaration of Independence and the principles embedded in it to provide the essential moral justifications for liberty, equality, and, of course, ending slavery—the natural and equal rights of the individual. Lincoln revered the Declaration and repeatedly quoted and referenced it in his speeches, debates, and writings before and after he became president. He used it again and again as a cudgel against the proslavery forces and slavery accommodationists. For example, on August 17, 1858, in Lewistown, Illinois, Lincoln delivered a powerful speech during his campaign for the U.S. Senate against Stephen A. Douglas, in which he verbally brandished the Declaration in his condemnation of slavery. Lincoln declared:

> Now, if slavery had been a good thing, would the Fathers of the Republic have taken a step calculated to diminish its beneficent influences among themselves, and snatch the boon wholly from their posterity? These communities [the colonies], by their representatives in old Independence Hall, said to the whole world of men: "We hold these truths to be self evident: that all men are created equal; that they are endowed by their Creator with certain unalienable rights; that among these are life, liberty and the pursuit of happiness." This was their majestic interpretation of the economy of the Universe. This was their lofty, and wise, and noble understanding of the justice of the Creator to His creatures. Yes, gentlemen, to all His creatures, to the whole great family of man.
>
> In their enlightened belief, nothing stamped with the Divine image and likeness was sent into the world to be trodden on, and degraded, and imbruted by its fellows. They grasped not only the whole race of man then living, but they reached forward and seized upon the farthest posterity. They erected a beacon to guide their children

and their children's children, and the countless myriads who should inhabit the earth in other ages. Wise statesmen as they were, they knew the tendency of prosperity to breed tyrants, and so they established these great self-evident truths, that when in the distant future some man, some faction, some interest should set up the doctrine that none but rich men, or none but white men, were entitled to life, liberty and the pursuit of happiness, their posterity might look up again to the Declaration of Independence and take course to renew the battle which their fathers began—so that truth, and justice, and mercy, and all the humane and Christian virtues might not be extinguished from the land; so that no man would hereafter dare to limit and circumscribe the great principles on which the temple of liberty was built.

Now, my countrymen, if you have been taught doctrines conflicting with the great landmarks of the Declaration of Independence; if you have listened to the suggestions which would take away from it grandeur, and mutilate the fair symmetry of its proportions; if you have been inclined to believe that all men are not created equal in those inalienable rights enumerated by our chart of liberty, let me entreat you to come back. Return to the fountain whose waters spring close by the blood of the Revolution. Think nothing of me—take no thought for the political fate of any man whomsoever—but come

> back to the truths that are in the Declaration of Independence.
>
> You may do anything with me you choose, if you will but heed these sacred principles. You may not only defeat me for the Senate, but you may take me and put me to death. While pretending no indifference to earthly honors, I do claim to be actuated in this contest by something higher than an anxiety for office. I charge you to drop every paltry and insignificant thought for any man's success. It is nothing; I am nothing; Judge Douglas is nothing. But do not destroy that immortal emblem of Humanity, the Declaration of American Independence.[25]

For Lincoln, the Declaration was a definitive statement about the spirit of the individual, morality, and humanity. Moreover, he considered it the essence of America's exceptionalism and extraordinary political system.

This brings us to the next step in understanding the American heritage—that is, natural rights in the context of natural law and the resulting civil society. Sir William Blackstone (1723–1780), among the most widely admired legal scholars often referred to by the Founders, wrote of natural law as "the foundation of what we call ethics . . . demonstrating that this or that action tends to man's real happiness, and therefore very justly concluding that the performance of it is a part of the law of nature; or, on the other hand, that this or that action is destruction of man's real happiness, and therefore that the law of nature forbids it."[26] He added: "The principal aim of society is to protect individuals, in the enjoyment of those absolute rights, which were vested in them by the immutable laws of nature; but which could not be preserved, in peace, without that mutual assistance, and intercourse, which is gained by the institution of friendly and social communities. Hence it follows, that the first and primary end of human laws, is to maintain and regulate these absolute rights of individuals."[27]

The late constitutional scholar and professor Chester James Antieau explained that Thomas Jefferson and his contemporaries also understood that in a civil society there are, by reason and necessity, natural law limitations on the exercise of natural rights. Jefferson said: "No man has a natural right to commit aggression on the equal rights of another." He added that "this is all from which the law ought to restrain him."[28] Jefferson also wrote: "Rightful liberty is unobstructed action according to our will within limits drawn around us by the equal rights of others."[29] Again, man has the ability, through right reason, to discern what is just, true, virtuous, and moral. But man is imperfect, and if he rejects reason for passion, irrationality, or worse, he is not free to harm or thwart the natural rights of another. Thus, as Antieau observed, "Natural law limitations upon the exercise of natural rights embrace in principle (1) consideration for the common good, (2) respect for the equal rights of others, and (3) realization that when the basis of the right is absent, the exercise of the claimed right can properly be denied."[30]

Therefore, natural law and the civil society or social order are not at odds with the individual's liberty but in harmony with it—each requiring the other.

The prominent British statesman and scholar Edmund Burke (1729–1797) emphasized another fundamental characteristic of the civil society—valuing human experience, tradition, and custom. Burke was outspoken in his sympathy for the American colonists and condemned the oppressions of the British monarchy that led to the American Revolution. However, he was also repulsed by the French Revolution. Burke saw the latter as a revolt led by elites and anarchists who had as their purpose not only redress against French rule but the utter destruction of French society, traditions, and customs. Burke explained: "There is a manifest, marked distinction, which ill men with ill designs, or weak men incapable of any design, will constantly be confounding,—that is, a marked distinction between change and reformation. The former alters the substance of the objects themselves, and gets rid of all their essential good as well as of all the accidental evil annexed to them. Change is novelty; and whether it is to operate any one of the effects of reformation at all, or whether it may not contradict the very principle upon which reformation is desired, cannot be known beforehand. Reform is not change in substance or in the primary modification of the object, but a direct application of a remedy to the grievance complained of. So far as that is removed, all is sure. It stops there; and if it fails, the substance which underwent the operation, at the very worst, is but where it was."[31] Burke added: "By this unprincipled facility of changing the state as often, and as much, and in as many ways, as there are floating fancies or fashions, the whole chain of continuity of the commonwealth would be broken. No one generation could link with the other. Men would become little better than the flies of a summer."[32]

Indeed, the Declaration sets forth this same understanding of reform over change: "Prudence, indeed, will dictate that Governments long established should not be changed for light and transient causes; and accordingly all experience hath shewn that mankind are more disposed to suffer, while evils are sufferable than to right themselves by abolishing the forms to which they are accustomed. But when a long train of abuses and usurpations, pursuing invariably the same Object, evinces a design to reduce them under absolute Despotism, it is their right, it is their duty, to throw off such Government, and to provide new Guards for their future security. Such has been the patient sufferance of these Colonies; and such is now the necessity which constrains them to alter their former Systems of Government. The history of the present King of Great Britain is a history of repeated injuries and usurpations, all having in direct object the establishment of an absolute Tyranny over these States."[33] Thereafter, the Founders list the specific injustices "to a candid world."[34]

TWO

# THE PROGRESSIVE MASTERMINDS

THE END OF THE nineteenth century saw the rise of a movement thoroughly hostile to the underlying principles of the nation's founding—the "Progressive Movement." Although I argued in *Liberty and Tyranny*,[1] *Ameritopia*,[2] and elsewhere that the term *Statist* better describes the left and its multifarious ideological forms and manifestations, it is impossible to decipher, unravel, and highlight certain aspects of the "progressive" history and influence on Americanism, and reference at some length its ideological founders and activists, without referring to it and them by the usual and accepted term. Therefore, for the purposes of this book I must do so out of convenience and necessity, albeit reluctantly.

Progressivism was imported from Europe and would result

in a radical break from America's heritage. In fact, it is best described as an elitist-driven counterrevolution to the American Revolution, in which the sovereignty of the individual, natural law, natural rights, and the civil society—built on a foundation of thousands of years of enlightened thinking and human experience—would be drastically altered and even abandoned for an ideological agenda broadly characterized as "historical progress."

Progressivism is the idea of the inevitability of historical progress and the perfectibility of man—and his self-realization—through the national community or collective. While its intellectual and political advocates clothe its core in populist terminology, and despite the existence of democratic institutions and cyclical voting, progressivism's emphasis on material egalitarianism and societal engineering, and its insistence on concentrated, centralized administrative rule, lead inescapably to varying degrees of autocratic governance. Moreover, for progressives there are no absolute or permanent truths, only passing and distant historical events. Thus even values are said to be relative to time and circumstances; there is no eternal moral order—that is, what was true and good in 1776 and before is not necessarily true and good today. Consequently, the very purpose of America's founding is debased.

To better understand this ideology, its refutation of the American heritage, and its enormous effect on modern American life, it is necessary to become acquainted with some of the most influential progressive intellectuals who, together with others, set the nation on this lamentable course. Given their prolific writings, it is neither possible nor necessary to delve into every manner of their thoughts or the differences among them in their brand of progressivism. For our purposes, it is enough to expose essential aspects of their arguments.

Herbert Croly (1869–1930) was among the leading academic and progressive thinkers. Croly cofounded the magazine *The New Republic* and authored *The Promise of American Life* (1909), an essential book among his fellow intellectuals, jurists, and certain powerful politicians, including Theodore Roosevelt. Among other things, Croly argued that "[t]o conceive the better American future as a consummation which will take care of itself,—as the necessary result of our customary conditions, institutions, and ideas,—persistence in such a conception is admirably designed to deprive American life of any promise at all. The better future which Americans propose to build is nothing if not an idea which must in certain essential respects emancipate them from their past. American history contains much matter for pride and congratulation, and much matter for regret and humiliation. . . . [Americans] must be prepared to sacrifice to that traditional vision even the traditional American ways of realizing it. Such a sacrifice is, I believe, coming to be demanded; and unless it is made, American life will gradually cease to have any specific Promise."[3]

Hence the American heritage and founding principles must be thrust aside if there is to be human progress. They are dismissed as outmoded and obstructive, impeding the pursuit of utopian ends, for they are unconnected to the present. Man, society, and the political and governing systems must be pliable to meet the special conditions of the day, subject to the commands of a consolidated and amalgamated ruling class. This requires a far-reaching change in education, the culture, and the American mind-set. In particular, the sacred rights of the individual, paramount under the Declaration of Independence's order, are said to be an old notion of individualism; they must give way to the new individualism—where the individual is subjugated to the mortal power of the state in the name of the general will and greater good.

Croly continued: "[T]he individual American will never obtain a sufficiently complete chance of self-expression, until the American nation has earnestly undertaken and measurably achieved the realization of its collective purpose. . . . [T]he cure for this individual sterility lies partly with the individual himself or rather with the man who proposes to become an individual; and under any plan of economic and social organization, the man who proposes to become an individual is a condition of the national as well as the individual improvement. It is none the less true that any success in the achievement of the national purpose will contribute positively to the liberation of the individual, both by diminishing his temptation, improving his opportunities, and by enveloping him in an invigorating rather than an enervating moral and intellectual atmosphere."[4]

More than a century later, in remarks delivered on July 13, 2012, President Barack Obama echoed Croly's sentiment: "[I]f you've been successful, you didn't get there on your own. . . . I'm always struck by people who think, well, it must be because I was just so smart. There are a lot of smart people out there. It must be because I worked harder than everybody else. Let me tell you something—there are a whole bunch of hardworking people out there. If you were successful, somebody along the line gave you some help. There was a great teacher somewhere in your life. Somebody helped to create this unbelievable American system that we have that allowed you to thrive. Somebody invested in roads and bridges. If you've got a business—you didn't build that. Somebody else made that happen. The Internet didn't get invented on its own. Government research created the Internet so that all the companies could make money off the Internet. The point is, is that when we succeed, we succeed because of our individual initiative, but also because we do things together. There are some things, just like fighting fires, we don't do on our own. I mean, imagine if everybody had their own fire service. That would be a hard way to organize fighting fires. So we say to ourselves, ever since the founding of this country, you know what, there are some things we do better together."[5]

Of course, no one is suggesting that individuals live in a bubble; certainly not the Founders or the philosophers who informed them. On the contrary, their dread was the deprivation of individual liberty and human rights by tyrannical governments of any form, but especially of the historically familiar centralized form.

Moreover, Croly, like many before and since, tied historic progress and the modern state to the idea of material egalitarianism, a central tenet of Marxism. Croly wrote: "It is the economic individualism of our existing national system which inflicts the most serious damage on American individuality; and American individual achievement in politics and science and the arts will remain partially impoverished as long as our fellow countrymen neglect or refuse systematically to regulate the distribution of wealth in the national interest. I am aware, of course, that the prevailing American conviction is absolutely contradictory of the foregoing assertion. Americans have always associated individual freedom with the unlimited popular enjoyment of all available economic opportunities. Yet it would be far more true to say that the popular enjoyment of practically unrestricted economic opportunities is precisely the condition which makes for individual bondage. . . ."[6]

In order to clear the way for the new progressive state—the fundamental objectives of which are largely antithetical to the American founding—its principles and institutions and the Founders themselves must therefore be disemboweled. In his book, *Progressive Democracy* (1914), Croly was blunt: "As in the case of every great political edifice, the materials composing the American system are derived from many different sources, and are characterized by unequal values, both as to endurance and as to latent possibilities. The appearance of definiteness and finality which it derives from its embodiment in specific constitutional documents and other authoritative words is to a large extent illusory. . . . Both historically and theoretically the American system is based upon an affirmation of popular political authority. When the colonists proclaimed their independence of the British Crown and Parliament, the repudiated sovereign had to be replaced with a capable substitute; and this substitute could consist under the circumstances only of the supposed makers of the Revolution—the American people as a whole. After the Declaration of Independence, the people, whoever they were and however their power was to be organized and expressed, became the only source of righteous political authority in the emancipated nation."[7] Croly went on: "Emphatic, however, as was this assertion of its direct control over its own political institutions by the primitive American democracy, its willingness to restrict its own effective political power was no less definite and insistent. It did not show the slightest disposition to translate this supposedly effective popular control over the institutes of government into active popular control over governmental behavior. The democracy abdicated the continuing active exercise of effective power in the very act of affirming the reality of its own ultimate legal authority."[8]

Besides, asserted Croly sarcastically, why should we revere the Founders, let alone surrender the present to their old and confining ideas and governmental designs? Not only were the

Founders imperfect, they were reacting to unique events at the time. Therefore, allegiance to their dated notions and governing construct constrains the natural flow of historical progress. "These early American democratic law-givers had no misgivings as to their own ability to draw up such a code. Both the political experience of their own forbears and a radical analysis of the origin of the meaning of society demonstrated the existence of certain individual rights as incontestable, indefeasible and inalienable as the right of the people to institute and alter their form of government. . . . The sacred words must be deposited in the ark of the covenant, there to remain inviolate as long as the commonwealth shall endure." Croly even raged against the Constitution's Bill of Rights: "By attempting to define a code of righteous political behavior, which could be enforced as law and which should be morally and legally binding on the people, the constitution makers were by way of depriving the sovereign of his own and necessary discretionary power. They did not merely associate popular political authority with the ideal law, but they tended to subordinate popular authority to an actual law. . . . The human will in its collective aspect was made subservient to the mechanism of a legal system."[9]

For Croly, the entire process of popular sovereignty exercised through representative republicanism, which led to the drafting, adoption, and ratification of the United States Constitution, was illegitimate, since it lacked direct popular voting. "In theory the fundamental Law should have been more completely the people's law . . . ; but in practice, the people have never had much to say about it. It was framed by a convention, the members of which were never expressly elected for the purpose by popular vote. It was ratified, not directly by the electorate, but by conventions which often represented only a small minority even of the legally qualified voters. In seeking to amend it the popular will could not act directly, but must get expressed through Congress and through state legislators and conventions. . . . The whole Federal system was by way of being an able, deliberate, beneficent and finally acceptable imposition on the people rather than an actual popular possession."[10]

Of course, the irony is that the kind of centralized administrative state Croly advocated, and which surrounds us today and is managed by a relative handful of architects, is all but immune from the popular will and completely impervious to direct popular sovereignty.

In a recurring theme among progressives, Croly condemned the Constitution's separation of powers, a doctrine essential to averting centralized tyranny, as the main obstacle to progress. "If the people are to be divided against themselves in order that righteousness may rule, still more must the government be divided against itself. It must be separated into departments each one of which must act independently of the others. . . . The government was prevented from doing harm, but in order that it might not do harm it was deliberately and effectively weakened. The people were protected from the government;

but quite as much was the government protected from the people. In dividing the government against itself by such high and rigid barriers, an equally substantial barrier was raised against the exercise by the people of any easy and sufficient control over their government. It was only a very strong and persistent popular majority which could make its will prevail, and if the rule of a majority was discouraged, the rule of a minority was equally encouraged. But the rulers, whether representing a majority or a minority, could not and were not supposed to accomplish much. It was an organization of obstacles and precautions—based at bottom on a profound suspicion of human nature."[11]

Furthermore, Croly was frustrated by legal restraints generally on governing as he continued to confound the unalienable rights of the individual (the supposed "old individualism" of the Declaration of Independence) with the liberating government authority of the state (the supposed "new individualism" manifested through the collective and general will). "Thus was instituted a system of representation by Law. Inasmuch as the ultimate popular political power was trustworthy only in case it were exercised, not merely through the medium of regular forms, but under rigid and effective limitations, the trustworthy agents of that power were not representative men exercising discretionary power, but principles of right which subordinated all officials to definite and binding restrictions. When the sovereign itself have implicitly surrendered its discretion to the Law, the personal agents of the sovereign can scarcely expect to retain theirs. The domination of the Law came to mean in practice a system in which the discretionary discriminatory purposive action of the human will in politics, whether collective or individual was suspect and should be reduced to the lowest practicable terms. The active government was divided, weakened, confined and deprived of integrity and effective responsibility, in order that a pre-established and authoritative Law might be exalted, confirmed and placed beyond the reach of danger."[12]

Consequently, Croly was not actually an advocate of popular sovereignty so much as he was an opponent of genuine individualism and constitutional republicanism, the latter two being obstacles to a centralized state in which it is claimed that governing authority exists at the behest of the people and for the good of the people. Let us remember, for the progressive, historical progress is said to be a process of never-ending cultural and societal adjustments intended to address the unique circumstances of the time, the ultimate goal of which is economic egalitarianism and the material liberation of "the masses." Unlike most of Europe, the American attitude, experience, and governing system were not compatible with the progressive ideology. Although Croly lamented the lack of direct democracy in America's founding, despite the open and active participation of the citizenry, he conveniently ignored that the people were never formally consulted or asked to approve the all-embracing counterrevolution and societal mutation of his progressive movement.

Like other progressives, Croly proclaimed a new secular "science," a *political and social science* in which politicians, bureaucrats, academics, and experts harness the power of the state to indoctrinate and rule over the individual, and attempt to remake his nature and society in general through constant experimentation and manipulation. This is said to be progress. Croly also argued that the American mind-set—the view of the "all-around man"—must be altered. The people must be conditioned to accept and then demand the kind of centralized administrative state he advocated. This is accomplished not only by demonizing the successful individual and, as he explained, demonstrating the benefits of administrative governance, but by producing like-minded believers through higher education. Croly wrote:

> Another condition must also be satisfied before an expert administration can expect to obtain popular confidence. Its authority will depend, as we have seen, on its ability to apply scientific knowledge to the realization of social purposes; and if a social science is unattainable or does not command popular respect, popular opinion will be reluctant to grant to the administration its necessary independent authority. Now in what way can a body of social knowledge be made to command popular respect? In the long run, doubtless, by increasing demonstration that social knowledge is the fruit of a binding and formative social ideal and that it is really serviceable for the accom-

> plishment of a social program. But is such a demonstration sufficient? Is there not another and equally necessary method of increasing popular confidence in the expert—the method of giving a much larger number of people the chance of acquiring a better intellectual training? Is it fair to ask millions of democrats to have a profound respect for scientific accomplishments whose possession is denied to them by the prevailing social and educational organization? It can hardly be claimed that the greater proportion of the millions who are insufficiently educated are not just as capable of being better educated as the thousands to whom science comes to have a real meaning. Society has merely deprived them of the opportunity. There may be certain good reasons for this negligence on the part of society; but as long as it exists, it must be recognized as in itself a good reason for the unpopularity of experts. The best way to popularize scientific administration, and to enable the democracy to consider highly educated officials as representatives, is to popularize the higher education. An expert administration cannot be sufficiently representative until it comes to represent a better educated constituency.[13]

Croly also condemned capitalism and private property rights. Writing in *The New Republic* on October 27, 1920, he asserted: "The unanswerable indictment against capitalism as an American institution is not that enterprising businessmen seized and exploited the opportunities and power which society placed at their disposal. It was natural and even necessary that they should organize production and distribution on a basis more profitable to themselves than to society. The offense against the American national welfare with which they are indictable is of a different kind. It is their blindness to the social penalties of their methods of hiring, firing and playing labor and their refusal to make the technical and social education of their employees a charge upon business or upon the businessman's state. . . ."[14] In this regard, Croly expressed the view held by all progressives, Democrat and Republican, in his era and since, that industrial America and, therefore, capitalism create an economic and social class system, different in specifics but not necessarily in kind to that described by Karl Marx (Marx's ideology to be discussed briefly later). Indeed, in condemning the progressivism of both major political parties as too tame, and encouraging support for a third party, the Farmer-Labor Party (essentially a socialist-workers' party), Croly complained that "[p]ractically all of the educational groundwork in public opinion for a Farmer-Labor party still remains to be done. Marxism Socialism has the advantage both of a definite creed and a Bible [*The Communist Manifesto*] which focuses the convictions and emotions of its adherents. . . ."[15] The overlap in the progressive and Marxist mind-set is simply inescapable.

Like most progressives, then and now, Croly became in-

creasingly frustrated with the supposed slow pace of the nation's transformation.

> As a progressive democrat whose faith survives the contemporary eclipse of progressivism, I am not willing to impute the triumph of unreformed and unrepentant party politics and economic privilege to the superior reality of their principles. It is due rather to the unreality which liberals have allowed to pervade liberalism. They have not studied the meaning of their experience and failures during the last twenty-five years. They have not as the result of this experience divined the need of adopting a more radical and realistic view of the nature and object of a liberal agitation under the conditions of American democracy. They accepted in the beginning and continue to accept certain assumptions about the seat of effective power in the American commonwealth and the relation between the state and social progress which condemn them to remain either the uneasy accomplices or the impotent enemies of the powers that be in American society. Progressives have assumed that the American commonwealth, as now instituted and operated, is a complete and essentially classless democracy whose citizens can cure its ailments and adjust its conflicts by virtue exclusively of political action, agitation and education. This assumption they share with their adversaries.

> It has falsified and will continue to falsify the American progressive movement. If progressives wish to vindicate their claim to serve as indispensable agents of American national fulfillment they will need to consciously abandon it.[16]

As will become clear, Croly was not alone in this outlook.

Incredibly, Theodore Roosevelt (1858–1919), America's twenty-sixth president (1901–1909), was a Croly admirer. Post-presidency, he was especially influenced by Croly's 1909 book, *The Promise of American Life*, which apparently was first drawn to his attention by Learned Hand, a very influential federal district judge, progressive, and a disciple of Croly's work. Hand wrote to Roosevelt: "I hope that you will find in it as comprehensive and progressive a statement of American Political ideas and ideals as I have found. I think that Croly has succeeded in stating more adequately than anyone else,—certainly of those writers whom I know,—the bases and prospective growth of the set of political ideas which can be fairly described as Neo-Hamilton, and whose promise is due more to you, as I believe, than to anyone else."[17]

On January 21, 1911, Roosevelt published an essay in the *Outlook*, where he was an associate editor, in which he wrote: "In Mr. Herbert Croly's *Promise of American Life*, the most profound and illuminating study of our National conditions which has appeared for many years, a special emphasis is laid on the assertion that the whole point of our governmental

experiment lies in the fact that it is a genuine effort to achieve true democracy—both political and industrial. The existence of this Nation has no real significance, from the standpoint of humanity at large, unless it means the rule of the people, and the achievement of a greater measure of widely diffused popular well-being than has ever before obtained on a like scale. . . ."[18]

A few months earlier, on August 31, 1910, Roosevelt gave his well-known "The New Nationalism" speech, widely admired and cited by modern progressives. The phrase—new nationalism—was actually coined not by Roosevelt but Croly.[19]

Like Croly and other progressives, Roosevelt dismantled and reinterpreted the Declaration of Independence, for he understood its principles stood as obstacles to the progressive mission. "In name we had the Declaration of Independence in 1776; but we gave the lie by our acts to the words of the Declaration of Independence until 1865; and words count for nothing except in so far as they represent acts. . . ."[20] Unlike an earlier Republican president, Abraham Lincoln, at no time during his speech did Roosevelt actually mention, let alone discuss, the Declaration's principles and their application to the nation and the Constitution. Nothing about "the Laws of Nature and of Nature's God," "a decent respect to the opinions of mankind," or that "We hold these truths to be self-evident, that all men are created equal, that they are endowed by their Creator with certain unalienable Rights, that among these are Life, Liberty and the pursuit of Happiness." Nor did Roosevelt note that Lincoln used the Declaration's principles, morality, and language as a foremost justification for prosecuting the Civil War and emancipating the slaves. In other words, the Declaration was the basis for moral and humane action. Had Roosevelt bothered to read from the Declaration's text, his distortion of the document as some kind of grant of or validation for immense federal governing authority would have collapsed.

In reality, Roosevelt attempted to both downplay the relevance of history, typical of the progressive approach, and use Lincoln and the Civil War to justify almost boundless modern interventions by the federal government in private life, especially the economy. "I do not speak of this struggle of the past merely from the historic standpoint. Our interest is primarily in the application today of the lessons taught by the contest of half a century ago. It is of little use for us to pay lip-loyalty to the mighty men of the past unless we sincerely endeavor to apply to the problems of the present precisely the qualities which in other crises enable the men of that day to meet those crises. It is half melancholy and half amusing to see the way in which well-meaning people gather to do honor to the man who, in company with John Brown, and under the lead of Abraham Lincoln, faced and solved the great problems of the nineteenth century, while, at the same time, these same good people nervously shrink from, or frantically denounce, those who are trying to meet the problems of the twentieth century in the spirit which was accountable for the successful solution of the problems of Lincoln's time."[21]

Of course, the new nationalism must dispose of the "old" federalism since the latter was to be a safeguard against exactly the kind of central authority Roosevelt boosted. Again, the progressive emphasizes simultaneously the "popular will" of the people and the centralization of governing power. "The New Nationalism puts the national need before sectional or personal advantage. It is impatient of the utter confusion that results from local legislatures attempting to treat national issues as local issues. It is still more impatient of the impotence which springs from overdivision of governmental powers, the impotence which makes it possible for local selfishness or for legal cunning, hired by wealthy special interests, to bring national activities to a deadlock. This New Nationalism regards the executive power as the steward of the public welfare. It demands of the judiciary that it shall be interested primarily in human welfare rather than in property, just as it demands that the representative body shall represent all the people rather than any one class or section of the people."[22]

And the concentration of governing authority has, as its purpose, the general welfare of the people. "The object of government is the welfare of the people. The material progress and prosperity of a nation are desirable chiefly so far as they lead to the moral and material welfare of all good citizens. Just in proportion as the average man and woman are honest, capable of sound judgment and high ideals, active in public affairs—but, first of all, sound in their home life, and the father and mother of healthy children whom they bring up well—just so far, and no farther, we may count our civilization a success. We must have—I believe we have already—a genuine and permanent moral awakening, without which no wisdom of legislation or administration really means anything; and, on the other hand, we must try to secure the social and economic legislation without which any improvement due to purely moral agitation is necessarily evanescent. Let me again illustrate by a reference to the Grand Army. You could not have won simply as a disorderly and disorganized mob. You needed generals; you needed careful administration of the most advanced type; and a good commissary—the cracker line. You well remember that success was necessary in many different lines in order to bring about general success."[23]

Roosevelt's attack on federalism, couched in populism, was both consistent and constant. For example, earlier, on August 29, 1910, speaking before the Colorado legislature, Roosevelt stated: "Unfortunately, the course of governmental construction by the courts, as also the course of governmental action by legislator and executive, has not kept pace in this nation during the last forty years with the extraordinarily complex industrial development. We have changed from what was predominately an agricultural people, where all were on planes of livelihood not far apart, and where business was simple, into a complex industrial community with a great development of corporations, and with conditions such that by steam and electricity the business of the nation has become completely nationalized. . . . Remember that I believe in state's rights wherever state's rights mean the people's rights. On the other hand, I believe in national rights wherever national rights mean the people's rights; and, above all, I believe in every part of our complicated social fabric there must be either national or state control, and that it is ruinous to permit governmental action . . . which prevents the exercise of such control. I am for a fact, not a formula; I am for the rights of the people first and foremost, and for the 'rights' of the nation or state, in any given series of cases, just in proportion as insistence upon them helps in securing popular rights."[24]

In 1912, after failing to win the Republican Party's nomination for president, Roosevelt formed a third party—the Progressive Party. Its platform stated, in part: "The Progressive Party, believing that a free people should have the power from time to time to amend their fundamental law so as to adapt it progressively to the changing needs of the people, pledges itself to provide a more easy and expeditious method of amending the Federal Constitution." "Up to the limit of the Constitution, and later by amendment of the Constitution, if found necessary, we advocate bringing under effective national jurisdiction those problems which have expanded beyond reach of the individual states." Moreover, it included a laundry list of proposed federal programs and policies covering health care, a minimum wage, retirement, education, etc.[25]

In the three-way presidential contest, Democrat Woodrow Wilson (1856–1924) was victorious, becoming the nation's twenty-eighth president, having won a plurality of the vote and a majority of the Electoral College vote. However, before ascending to the Oval Office, Wilson was one of the nation's leading intellectual proponents of progressivism and its counterrevolution. In his writings and speeches, Wilson repeatedly took aim at the Declaration of Independence's stated principles, but with even greater force and contempt than Roosevelt.

In 1907, in a Fourth of July address about the Declaration, Wilson, then president of Princeton University, wrote:

> It is common to think of the Declaration of Independence as a highly speculative document; but no one can think it so who has read it. It is a strong, rhetorical statement of grievances against the English government. It does indeed open with the assertion that all men are equal and that they have certain inalienable rights, among them the right to life, liberty and the pursuit of happiness. It asserts that governments were instituted to secure these rights, and can derive their just powers only from the consent of the governed; and it solemnly declares that "whenever any government becomes destructive of these ends, it is the right of the people to alter or to abolish it, and to institute a new government, laying its foundations in such principles, and organizing its powers in such forms, as to them shall seem most likely to

effect their safety and happiness." But this would not afford a general theory of government to formulate policies upon. No doubt we are meant to have liberty, but each generation must form its own conception of what liberty is. No doubt we shall always wish to be given leave to pursue happiness as we will, but we are not yet sure where or by what method we shall find it. That we are free to adjust government to these ends we know. But Mr. Jefferson and his colleagues in the Continental Congress prescribed the law of adjustment for no generation but their own. They left us to say whether we thought the government they had set up was founded on "such principles," its powers organized in "such forms" as seemed to us most likely to effect our safety and happiness. They did not attempt to dictate the aims and objects of any generation but their own. . . .[26]

Wilson added:

So far as the Declaration of Independence was a theoretical document, that is its theory. Do we still hold it? Does the doctrine of the Declaration of Independence still live in our principles of action, in the things we do, in the purposes we applaud, in the measures we approve? It is not a question of piety. We are not bound to adhere to the doctrines held by the signers of the Declaration of Independence; we are as free as they were to make and

> unmake governments. We are not here to worship men or a document. But neither are we here to indulge in a mere rhetorical and uncritical eulogy. Every Fourth of July should be a time for examining our standards, our purposes, for determining afresh what principles, what forms of power we think most likely to effect our safety and happiness. That and that alone is the obligation the Declaration lays upon us. It is no fetish; its words lay no compulsion upon the thought of any free man; but it was drawn by men who thought, and it obliges those who receive its benefits to think likewise. . . .[27]

In May 1908, Wilson authored a paper titled "Constitutional Government in the United States." He flatly denounced the principles both explicit and inherit in America's founding. He declared: "No doubt a great deal of nonsense has been talked about the inalienable rights of the individual, and a great deal that was mere vague sentiment and pleasing speculation has been put forward as fundamental principle."[28]

On May 12, 1911, Wilson spoke to the Jefferson Club of Los Angeles, where he again voiced his contempt for the essence of America's founding document: "I am constantly reminding audiences . . . that the rhetorical introduction of the Declaration of Independence is the least part of it. That was the theoretical expression of the views of which the rest of the document was meant to give teeth and substance to. The Declaration . . . is a long enumeration of the issues of the year 1776, of exactly the things that were then supposed to be radical matters of discontent among the people living in America—the things which they meant to remedy in the spirit of the introductory paragraphs, but which the introductory paragraphs themselves did not contain. . . ."[29]

On July 4, 1914, when actually speaking at Independence Hall, then-president Wilson declared:

> Have you ever read the Declaration of Independence or attended with close comprehension to the real character of it when you have heard it read? If you have, you will know that it is not a Fourth of July oration. The Declaration of Independence was a document preliminary to war. It was a vital piece of practical business, not a piece of rhetoric; and if you will pass beyond those preliminary passages which we are accustomed to quote about the rights of men and read into the heart of the document you will see that it is very express and detailed, that it consists of a series of definite specifications concerning actual public business of the day. Not the business of our day, for the matter with which it deals is past, but the business of that first revolution by which the Nation was set up, the business of 1776. Its general statements, its general declarations cannot mean anything to us unless we append to it a similar specific body of particulars as to what we consider the essential business of our own day. . . .
>
> Liberty does not consist, my fellow-citizens, in mere

general declarations of the rights of man. It consists in the translation of those declarations into definite action. Therefore, standing here where the declaration was adopted, reading its businesslike sentences, we ought to ask ourselves what there is in it for us. There is nothing in it for us unless we can translate it into the terms of our own conditions and of our own lives. We must reduce it to what the lawyers call a bill of particulars. It contains a bill of particulars, but the bill of particulars of 1776. If we would keep it alive, we must fill it with a bill of particulars of the year 1914. . . .

In one sense the Declaration of Independence has lost its significance. It has lost its significance as a declaration of national independence. Nobody outside of America believed when it was uttered that we could make good our independence; now nobody anywhere would dare to doubt that we are independent and can maintain our independence. As a declaration of independence, therefore, it is a mere historic document. Our independence is a fact so stupendous that it can be measured only by the size and energy and variety and wealth and power of one of the greatest nations in the world. But it is one thing to be independent and it is another thing to know what to do with your independence.[30]

As if directly admonishing the late Wilson, on July 5, 1926, the thirtieth president, Calvin Coolidge, delivered his own speech in Philadelphia about the Declaration's meaning. He stated:

> The American Revolution represented the informed and mature convictions of a great mass of independent, liberty loving, God-fearing people who knew their rights, and possessed the courage to dare to maintain them. . . .
>
> The Continental Congress was not only composed of great men, but it represented a great people. While its Members did not fail to exercise a remarkable leadership, they were equally observant of their representative capacity. They were industrious in encouraging their constituents to instruct them to support independence. But until such instructions were given they were inclined to withhold action. . . .
>
> A spring will cease to flow if its source be dried up; a tree will wither if its roots be destroyed. In its main features the Declaration of Independence is a great spiritual document. It is a declaration not of material but of spiritual conceptions. Equality, liberty, popular sovereignty, the rights of man—these are not elements which we can see and touch. They are ideals. They have their source and their roots in the religious convictions. They belong to the unseen world. Unless the faith of the American people in these religious convictions is to endure, the principles of our Declaration will perish. We cannot continue to enjoy the result if we neglect and abandon the cause.

We are too prone to overlook another conclusion. Governments do not make ideals, but ideals make governments. This is both historically and logically true. Of course the government can help to sustain ideals and can create institutions through which they can be the better observed, but their source by their very nature is in the people. The people have to bear their own responsibilities. There is no method by which that burden can be shifted to the government. It is not the enactment, but the observance of laws, that creates the character of a nation.

About the Declaration there is a finality that is exceedingly restful. It is often asserted that the world has made a great deal of progress since 1776, that we have had new thoughts and new experiences which have given us a great advance over the people of that day, and that we may therefore very well discard their conclusions for something more modern. But that reasoning cannot be applied to this great charter. If all men are created equal, that is final. If they are endowed with inalienable rights, that is final. If governments derive their just powers from the consent of the governed, that is final. No advance, no progress can be made beyond these propositions. If anyone wishes to deny their truth or their soundness, the only direction in which he can proceed historically is not forward, but backward toward the time when there was no equality, no rights of the individual,

> no rule of the people. Those who wish to proceed in that direction cannot lay claim to progress. They are reactionary. Their ideas are not more modern, but more ancient, than those of the Revolutionary fathers. . . .[31]

The danger of rejecting America's founding principles is illustrated best in this instance by Wilson himself. As is well documented, Wilson was an open racist who, among other things, as president resegregated the federal bureaucracy.[32]

Therefore, while Lincoln embraced the Declaration of Independence before and during the Civil War to justify both prosecuting the war and abolishing slavery, Wilson denounced the same principles and language in the Declaration as nonsense or dismissed them as relevant only to the American Revolution, insisting that to treat them as the Founders intended served as an impediment to communal progress.

In 1913, Wilson wrote *The New Freedom*, in which he proclaimed, "We are in the presence of a new organization of society. Our life has broken away from the past. The life of America is not the life that it was twenty years ago; it is not the life that it was ten years ago. We have changed our economic conditions, absolutely, from top to bottom; and, with our economic society, the organization of our life. The old political formulas do not fit the present problems; they read now like documents taken from a forgotten age. The older cries sound as if they belonged to a past age which men have almost forgotten. . . ."[33] "We used to think in the old-fashioned days when life was very simple that all that government had to do was to put on a policeman's uniform, and say, 'Now don't anybody hurt anybody else.' We used to say that the idea of government was for every man to be left alone and not interfered with, except when he interfered with somebody else; and that the best government was the government that did as little governing as possible. That was the idea that obtained in Jefferson's time. But we are coming now to realize that life is so complicated that we are not dealing with the old conditions, and that the law has to step in and create new conditions under which we may live, the conditions which will make it tolerable for us to live."[34]

America is more complex and thus the federal government should become more complex? Life is more complicated, compelling a more complicated federal government? And the more complex and complicated life and society, the greater justification for centralized governmental decision making? This is a common theme among progressive intellectuals, past and present. However, is this approach not counterintuitive given the long and cruel history of authoritarianism? Wilson added: "I am, therefore, forced to be a progressive, if for no other reason, because we have not kept up with our changes of conditions, either in the economic field or in the political field. We have not kept up as well as other nations have. We have not kept our practices adjusted to the facts of the case, and until we do, and unless we do, the facts of the case will always have the better argument; because if you do not adjust your laws to the facts, so much the worse for the law, not for the facts, because law trails along after the facts. Only that law is unsafe which runs ahead of the facts and beckons to it and make it follow the will-o'-the-wisps of imaginative projects."[35]

Again, what are the limits of the progressive's government? Wilson saw few. "I believe the time has come when the governments of this country, both state and national, have to set the stage, and set it very minutely and carefully, for the doing of justice to men in every relationship of life. It has been free and easy with us so far; it has been go as you please; it has been every man look out for himself; and we have continued to assume, up to this year when every man is dealing, not with another man, in most cases, but with a body of men whom he has not seen, that the relationships of property are the same that they always were. We have great tasks before us, and we must enter on them as befits men charged with the responsibility of shaping a new era."[36]

The goal is nothing less than the perfectibility of man, above all his economic condition (meaning, equitable distribution of wealth), through unbounded activist government. "Human freedom consists in perfect adjustments of human interests and human activities and human energies. Now, the adjustments necessary between individuals, between individuals and the complex institutions amidst which they live, and between those institutions and the government, are infinitely more intricate today than ever before. No doubt this is a tiresome and roundabout way of saying the same thing, yet perhaps it is worthwhile to get somewhat clearly in our mind what makes all the trouble today. Life has become complex; there are many more elements, more parts, to it than ever before. And, therefore, it is harder to keep everything adjusted,—and harder to find out where the trouble lies when the machine gets out of order."[37]

Wilson's distrust of republican government, and his belief in rule by a trained centralized bureaucracy, independent from the genuine consent of the governed and constitutional constraints, should come as no surprise. In 1886, while teaching at Bryn Mawr College, Wilson penned an essay titled "Study of Public Administration." He declared that debates about "who shall make the law, and what shall that law be" was simply "the philosophy of any time is, as [Georg Wilhelm Friedrich] Hegel says, 'nothing but the spirit of that time expressed in abstract thought'; and political philosophy, like philosophy of every other kind, had only held up the mirror to contemporary affairs. . . . There was little or no trouble about administration—at least little that was heeded by administrators."[38] Again, for Wilson and the progressives, the American founding was simply a historical event distinct to its own moment and condition. Progress requires that America not get stuck in its own history. "In brief, if difficulties of governmental action are to be seen gathering in other centuries, they are to be seen culminating in our own. This is the reason why administrative tasks have nowadays to be so studiously and systematically adjusted to carefully tested standards of policy, the reason why we are having now what we never had before, a science of administration. The weightier debates of constitutional principle are even yet by no means concluded; but they are no longer of more immediate practical moment than questions of administration. It is getting to be harder to run a constitution than to frame one."[39]

Where are we to find this science of administration? It is to be imported from Europe. "It has found its doctors in Europe. It is not of our making; it is a foreign science, speaking very little of the language of English or American principle. It employs only foreign tongues; it utters none but what are to our minds alien ideas. Its aims, its examples, its conditions, are almost exclusively grounded in the histories of foreign races, in the precedents of foreign systems, in the lessons of foreign revolutions. It has been developed by French and German professors, and is consequently in all parts adapted to the needs of a compact state, and made to fit highly centralized forms of government. . . . If we employ it, we must Americanize it, and that not formally, in language merely, but radically, in thought, principle, and aim as well. . . ."[40]

And the people cannot be bothered with administration, for not only are they too busy, but they are simply unfit for and incapable of such a momentous task. It must be left to a relative handful of sensible and learned professionals. "In government, as in virtue, the hardest of hard things is to make progress. Formerly the reason for this was that the single person who was sovereign was generally selfish, ignorant, timid, or a fool—albeit there was now and again one who was wise. Nowadays the reason is that the many, the people, who are sovereign have no single ear which one can approach, and are selfish, ignorant, timid, stubborn, or foolish with the selfishnesses, the ignorances, the stubbornesses, the timidities, or the follies of several thousand persons—albeit there are hundreds who are wise."[41] "The bulk of mankind is rigidly unphilosophical, and nowadays the bulk of mankind votes."[42]

Moreover, the bureaucracy will be of the noblest and most virtuous sort, with no personal, political, or ideological agenda, motivated solely and completely by its technical know-how in and public-spiritedness for the general good and welfare. "It will be necessary to organize democracy by sending up to the competitive examinations for civil service men definitely prepared for standing liberal tests as to technical knowledge. A technically schooled civil service will presently have become indispensable. I know that a corps of civil servants prepared by a special schooling and drilled, after appointment, into a perfected organization, with appropriate hierarchy and characteristic discipline, seems to a great many very thoughtful persons to contain elements which might combine to make an offensive official class. . . . But to fear the creation of a domineering illiberal officialism as a result of the studies I am here proposing is to miss altogether the principle upon which I wish most to insist. That principle is, that administration in the United States must be at all points sensitive to public opinion. . . ." At the same time, however, Wilson insisted that "[s]teady, hearty allegiance to the policy of government they serve will constitute good behavior. That *policy* will have no taint of officialdom about it. . . . Bureaucracy can exist only where the whole service of the state is removed from the common political life of the people, its chiefs as well as its rank and file. Its motives, its objects, its policy, its standards, must be bureaucratic. . . ."[43]

Unsurprisingly, but significantly, Wilson insisted that the centralized administrative state must, by logic and necessity, replace or thoroughly alter the constitutional structure—particularly the Framers' incorporation of Charles de Montesquieu's separation-of-powers doctrine, essential to curtailing the likelihood of concentrated tyranny, which must be abandoned in principle. Otherwise there can be no real historical progress. "The study of administration, philosophically viewed, is closely connected with the study of the proper distribution of constitutional authority. . . . If administrative study can discover the best principles upon which to base such distribution, it will have done constitutional study an invaluable service. Montesquieu did not, I am convinced, say the last word on this head."[44] Hence the administrative state is to effectively replace the constitutional state, the latter being old and immovable.

This brings us to John Dewey (1859–1952), among the foremost progressive thinkers. Dewey, like Croly and Wilson, among others, claimed that progressivism was, in essence, a science-based pragmatism. Like most progressives, he also argued that there is no timeless, absolute truth since all things are subject to change and situation. Therefore, he also unremittingly condemned John Locke and the Declaration of Independence, and the idea of permanent truths, a transcendent moral order, and individual natural rights. In his 1935 book, *Liberalism and Social Action*, Dewey wrote:

> The outstanding points of Locke's version of liberalism are that governments are instituted to protect the rights that belong to individuals prior to political organization and social relations. The rights are those summed up a century later in the American Declaration of Independence: the rights of life, liberty and the pursuit of happiness. . . . The whole temper of this philosophy is individualistic in the sense in which individualism is opposed to organized social action. It held to the primacy of the individual over the state not only in time but in moral authority. It defined the individual in terms of liberties of thought and action already possessed by him in some mysterious ready-made fashion, and which it was the sole business of the state to safeguard. Reason was also made an inherent endowment of the individual, expressed in men's moral relations to one another, but not sustained and developed because of these relations. It followed that the great enemy of individual liberty was thought to be government because of its tendency to encroach upon the innate liberties of individuals. Later

> liberalism inherited this conception of a natural antagonism between the individual and organized society. There still lingers in the minds of some the notion that there are two different "spheres" of action and of rightful claims; that of political society and that of the individual, and that in the interest of the latter the former must be as contracted as possible. Not till the second half of the nineteenth century did the idea arise that government might and should be an instrument for securing and extending the liberties of individuals. . . .[45]

Further dismissing the purpose of the founding, with its emphasis on the individual, Dewey continued: "The ideas of Locke embodied in the Declaration of Independence were congenial to our pioneer conditions that gave individuals the opportunity to carve out their own careers. Political action was lightly thought of by those who lived in frontier conditions. A political career was very largely annexed as an adjunct to the action of individuals in carving their own careers."[46]

Moreover, Dewey was a stern critic of capitalism and private property rights, which he condemned as a relic of early American principles reinforced in current times by the political party structure. On March 18, 1931, in *The New Republic*, Dewey wrote: "I do not mean that the whole alliance of the [political] parties with organized business is consciously sinister and corrupt, though it is easily demonstrable that this is somewhat true. I mean rather that both old parties represent that stage of American life when the American people as a whole felt that society was to advance by means of industrial inventions and their application; by the development of manufacturing, of railways and commerce. It was that stage of American life when all but a few took for granted the natural control of industry and trade by the profit motive and the necessity of accumulating money capital. This idea may once have played a part in the development of the country. It has now ceased to be anything but an obstruction. . . ."[47]

In his 1930 book, *Individualism Old and New,* Dewey acknowledged Marx's influence on him and progressivism: "[T]he issue which [Marx] raised—the relation of the economic structure to political operations—is one that actively persists. Indeed, it forms the only basis of present political questions. An intelligent and experienced observer of affairs at Washington has said that all political questions which he has heard discussed in Washington come back ultimately to problems connected with the distribution of income. Wealth, property and processes of manufacturing and distribution—down to retail trade through the chain system—can hardly be socialized in outward effect without political repercussion. It constitutes an ultimate issue which must be faced by new and existing political parties. There is still enough vitality in the older individualism to offer a very serious handicap to any party or program which calls itself by the name of Socialism. . . ."[48] "We are in for some kind of socialism, call it by whatever name we please, and no matter what it will be called when it is realized.

Economic determinism is now a fact, not a theory. But there is a difference and a choice between a blind, chaotic and unplanned determinism, issuing from business conducted for pecuniary profit, and the determination of a socially planned and ordered development. It is the difference and the choice between a socialism that is public and one that is capitalistic."[49]

Dewey criticized Marx's call for the violent overthrow of the status quo. However, Dewey insisted that the present attachment to the principles and values of the American founding must be repudiated and replaced with the new scientific approach, which he argued addresses the modern social conditions of the collective. "The scientific attitude is experimental as well as intrinsically communicative. If it were generally applied, it would liberate us from the heavy burden imposed by dogmas and external standards. Experimental method is something other than the use of blow-pipes, retorts and reagents. It is the foe of every belief that permits habit and wont to dominate invention and discovery, and ready-made system to override verifiable fact. Constant revision is the work of experimental inquiry. By revision of knowledge and ideas, power to effect transformation is given us. This attitude, once incarnated in the individual mind, would find an operative outlet. If dogmas and institutions tremble when a new idea appears, this shiver is nothing to what would happen *if the idea were armed with the means for the continuous discovery of new truth and the criticism of old belief*. To 'acquiesce' in science is dangerous only for those who would maintain affairs in the existing social order unchanged because of lazy habit or self-interest. For the scientific attitude demands faithfulness to whatever is discovered and steadfastness in adhering to new truth."[50]

Dewey's appeal to and faith in the social sciences is akin to a religious fundamentalism. "The destructive effect of science upon beliefs long cherished and values once prized is, and quite naturally so, a great cause of dread of science and its application in life. The law of inertia holds of the imagination and its loyalties as truly as of physical things. I do not suppose that it is possible to turn suddenly from these negative effects to possible positive and constructive ones. But as long as we refuse to make an effort to change the direction which imagination looks at the world, as long as we remain unwilling to reexamine old standards and values, science will continue to wear its negative aspect. Take science . . . for what it is, and we shall begin to envisage it as a potential creator of new values and ends. We shall have an intimation, on a wide and generous scale, of the release, the increased initiative, independence and inventiveness, which science now brings in its own specialized fields to the individual scientist. It will be seen as a means of originality and individual variation. . . ."[51]

Acceptance of the social sciences and experimentation, without the inhibitions of old beliefs, is intended to achieve a new individuality with real freedom, shaped by present events and surroundings. "Individuality is at first spontaneous and unshaped; it is a potentiality, a capacity of development. Even so, it is a unique manner of acting in and with a world of objects and persons. It is not something complete in itself. . . . Since individuality is a distinctive way of feeling the impacts of the world and of showing a preferential bias in response to these impacts, it develops into shape and form only through interaction with actual conditions; it is no more complete in itself than is a painter's tube of paint without relation to a canvas. . . . In its determination, the potential individuality of the artist takes on visible and enduring forms. The imposition of individuality as something made in advance always gives evidence of a mannerism, not a manner; something formed in the very process of creation of other things. The future is always unpredictable. Ideals, including that of a new and effective individuality, must themselves be framed out of the possibilities of existing conditions, even if these be the conditions that constitute a corporate and industrial age. The ideals take shape and gain a content as they operate in remaking conditions. We may, in order to have continuity of direction, plan a program of action in anticipation of occasions as they emerge. But a program of ends and ideals if kept apart from sensitive and flexible method becomes an encumbrance. For its hard and rigid character assumes a fixed world and a static individual; and neither of these things exists. It implies that we can prophesy the future—an attempt which terminates, as someone has said, in prophesying the past or in its reduplication."[52]

In 1934, Dewey delivered a speech, "The Future of Liberalism," in which he declared: "The commitment of liberalism to experimental procedure carries with it the idea of continuous reconstruction of the ideas of individuality and of liberty, in their intimate connection with changes in social relations. It is enough to refer to the changes in productivity and distribution since the time when the earlier liberalism was formulated, and the effect of these transformations, due to science and technology, upon the terms on which men associate together. An experimental method is the recognition of this temporal change in ideas and policies so that the latter may coordinate with the facts, instead of being opposed to them. Any other view maintains a rigid conceptualism, and implies that facts should conform to concepts that are framed independently of temporal or historical change."[53]

The work of the social scientists—in and out of government—is inexhaustible. Social experimentation is continuous and, if need be, sweeping.

> Experimental method is not just messing around nor doing a little of this and a little of that in the hope that things will improve. Just as in the physical sciences, it implies a coherent body of ideas, a theory, that gives direction to effort. What is implied, in contrast to every form of absolutism is that the ideas and theory be taken as methods of action tested and continuously revised by the consequences they produce in actual social conditions. Since they are operational in nature, they modify conditions, while the first requirement, that of basing policies upon realistic study of actual conditions, brings

> about their continuous reconstruction. It follows finally that there is no opposition in principle between liberalism as social philosophy and radicalism in action, if by radicalism is signified the adoption of policies that bring about drastic, instead of piecemeal, social change. It is all a question of what kind of procedures an intelligent study of changing conditions discloses. These changes have been so tremendous in the last century, yes, in the last forty years, that it looks to me as if radical methods were now necessary. But all that the argument here requires is recognition of the fact that there is nothing in the nature of liberalism that makes it a milk-water doctrine, committed to compromise and minor "reforms." It is worth noting that the earlier liberals were regarded in their day as subversive radicals.[54]

Indeed, Dewey insisted that the progressive ideology is more than a governing ideology. It must reverberate throughout all corners of society. "[T]he full freedom of the human spirit and of individuality can be achieved only as there is effective opportunity to share in the cultural resources of civilization. No economic state of affairs is merely economic. It has a profound effect upon the presence or absence of cultural freedom. Any liberalism that does not make full cultural freedom supreme and that does not see the relation between it and genuine industrial freedom as a way of life is a degenerate and delusive liberalism."[55]

In fact, Dewey was an early advocate of reconstructing education to comport with his notions of progressivism and integrate his ideology into the public school system. He was a renowned education "innovator" whose influence throughout academia remains considerable to this day. Dewey argued against merely teaching basic academic coursework, which both teacher and student are to transcend. Instead, education is to emphasize the general consciousness for the social community and collective, focusing on the student's (whom he called "the immature") psychological development in this regard—cognition not of individual thought but groupthink. Of course, the student is discouraged from absorbing the truths, traditions, and customs of the past and rather is encouraged to be pragmatic, flexible, and experimental. In his 1916 book, *Democracy and Education*, Dewey argued:

> It remains only to point out . . . that the reconstruction of experience may be social as well as personal. For purposes of simplification we have spoken . . . as if the education of the immature which fills them with the spirit of the social group to which they belong, were a sort of catching up of the child with the aptitudes and resources of the adult group. In static societies, societies which make the maintenance of established custom their measure of value, this conception applies in the main. But not in progressive communities. They endeavor to shape the experiences of the young so that instead of repro-

> ducing current habits, better habits shall be formed, and thus the future adult society be an improvement on their own. Men have long had some intimation of the extent to which education may be consciously used to eliminate obvious social evils through starting the young on paths which shall not produce these ills, and some idea of the extent in which education may be made an instrument of realizing the better hopes of men. But we are doubtless far from realizing the potential efficacy of education as a constructive agency of improving society, from realizing that it represents not only a development of children and youth but also of the future society of which they will be the constituents.[56]

Dewey condemned the existing approach to education for lacking socialization and the scientific inquiry he demanded:

> The pupil learns symbols without the key to their meaning. He acquires a technical body of information without ability to trace its connections with the objects and operations with which he is familiar—often he acquires simply a peculiar vocabulary. There is a strong temptation to assume that presenting subject matter in its perfected form provides a royal road to learning. What more natural than to suppose that the immature can be saved time and energy, and be protected from needless error by commencing where competent inquirers have left off?

> The outcome is written large in the history of education. Pupils begin their study of science with texts in which the subject is organized into topics according to the order of the specialist. Technical concepts, with their definitions, are introduced at the outset. Laws are introduced at a very early stage, with at best a few indications of the way in which they were arrived at. The pupils learn a "science" instead of learning the scientific way of treating familiar material of ordinary experience. The method of the advanced student dominates college teaching; the approach of the college is transferred into the high school, and so down the line, with such omissions as may make the subject easier. . . .[57]

What, then, should students be taught? "The problem of an education use of science is then to create an intelligence pregnant with belief in the possibility of the direction of human affairs by itself. The method of science engrained through education in habit means emancipation from rule of thumb and from the routine generated by rule of thumb procedure. . . . Under the influence of conditions created by the non-existence of experimental science, experience was opposed in all the ruling philosophies of the past to reason and the truly rational. Empirical knowledge meant the knowledge accumulated by a multitude of past instances without intelligent insight into the principles of any of them. . . . Science is experience becoming rational. The effect of science is thus to change men's idea of the nature and inherent possibilities of experience. . . . Science carries on its working over of prior subject matter on a large scale. It aims to free an experience from all which is purely personal and strictly immediate; it aims to detach whatever it has in common with the subject matter of other experiences, and which, being common, may be saved for further use. It is, thus, an indispensable factor in social progress. In any experience just as it occurs there is much which, while it may be of precious import to the individual implicated in the experience, is peculiar and unreduplicable. From the standpoint of science, this material is accidental, while the features which are widely shared are essential. . . . In emancipating an idea from the particular context in which it originated and giving it a wider reference the results of the experience of any individual are put at the disposal of all men. Thus ultimately and philosophically, science is the organ of general social progress. . . ."[58]

Dewey's advocacy of education as a means to socialize a nation's youth toward a collectivist social and economic mentality was in keeping with his glowing critique of the Soviet Union's approach to education a few years earlier. After visiting the Soviet Union, on December 5, 1928, Dewey wrote in *The New Republic* that "in the 'transitional' state of Russia chief significance attaches to the mental and moral (*pace* the Marxians) change that is taking place; that while in the end this transformation is supposed to be a means to economic and political change, for the present it is the other way around.

This consideration is equivalent to saying that the import of all institutions is educational in the broad sense—that of their effects upon disposition and attitude. Their function is to create habits so that persons will act cooperatively and collectively as readily as now in capitalistic countries they act 'individualistically.' The same consideration defines the importance and the purpose of the narrower education agencies, the schools. They represent a direct and concentrated effort to obtain the effect which other institutions develop in a diffused and roundabout manner. The schools are, in current phase, the 'ideological arm of the Revolution.' In consequence, the activities of the schools dovetail in the most extraordinary way, both in administrative organization and in aim and spirit, into all other social agencies and interests."[59] Dewey continued: "During the transitional regime, the school cannot count upon the larger education to create in any single and wholehearted way the required collective and cooperative mentality. The traditional customs and institutions of the peasant, his small tracts, his three-system farming, the influence of home and Church, all work automatically to create in him an individualistic ideology. In spite of the greater inclination of the city worker towards collectivism, even his social environment works adversely in many respects. Hence the great task of the school is to counteract and transform those domestic and neighborhood tendencies that are still so strong, even in a nominally collectivist regime."[60]

Walter Weyl (1873–1919) was another dominant progressive voice and strong nationalist. He opened his 1912 book, *The New Democracy*, with a withering attack on early-twentieth-century America, followed by a cynical manipulation of the American founding. "America today is in a somber, soul-questioning mood. We are in a period of clamor, of bewilderment, of an almost tremulous unrest. We are hastily revising all our social conceptions. We are hastily testing all our political ideals. We are profoundly disenchanted with the fruits of a century of dependence. . . . It is in this moment of misgiving, when men are beginning to doubt the all-efficiency of our old-time democracy, that a new democracy is born. It is a new spirit, critical, concrete, insurgent. A clear-eyed discontent is abroad in the land. . . ."[61]

Weyl continued: "In reality the democracy of 1776 was by no means perfect. The Declaration of Independence was not an organic law, but an appeal—a very special and adroit appeal—to the 'natural right' of revolution. It was a beautiful ideal, as wonderfully poised in mid-air as is today the golden rule among the thrice-armed nations of Europe. The average American was not a true believer in its doctrines. The 'better classes,' tainted with an interested loyalty to King George, could not abide rebels, petitioners, and 'agitators,' and among the signers were many conservative men who feared 'too much democracy,' although they saw the advantage of issuing a 'platform,' and of hanging together to avoid 'hanging separately.'"[62] "America in 1776 was not a democracy. It was not even a democracy on paper. It was at best a shadow-democracy. Nor was the substance of democracy conferred by the federal Constitution. If our modern ideal of democracy does not lead back to the noble eloquence of the Declaration, still less does it revert to the federal Constitution, as it issued, in 1787, fresh from the Philadelphia Convention. Our newer democracy demands, not that the people forever conform to a rigid, hard-charging Constitution, but that the Constitution change to conform to the people. The Constitution is the political wisdom of dead America."[63]

In fact, wrote Weyl: "So intimately has this Constitution been bound up with our dearest national ideals and with our very sense of national unity, so many have been the gentle traditions which have clustered about this venerable document, that one hesitates to apply to it the ordinary canons of political criticism. For over a century we have piously exclaimed that our Constitution is the last and noblest expression of democracy. But, in truth, the Constitution is not democratic. It was, in intention, and is, in essence, undemocratic. It was conceived in violent distrust of the common people. . . ."[64] "The greatest merit—and the greatest defect—of the Constitution is that it has survived. It might be well if the American people would recast their Constitution every generation. We would assuredly do better in 1911 with a twentieth century organic law than with an almost unchangeable constitution, which antedated the railroad, the steamboat, and the French Revolution, and was contemporary with George the Third, Marie Antoinette, and the flintlock muskets. In the early days, however, when the States were jealous, exigent, and eternally over vigilant, any bond of union, if only strong enough, was good. . . ."[65]

Again and again, the goal of the progressives is to unmoor the individual and society from America's heritage with populist tirades, prodding, and indoctrination, the purpose of which is to build popular support for a muscular centralized government ruled by a self-aggrandizing intellectual elite through an extraconstitutional and autocratic administrative Leviathan. Moreover, the individual is to be denuded of his personal traits, "primitive nature," and "old beliefs," since his true liberty, satisfaction, and realization are said to be tied to the universality of the state. The government, through "science" and administration—unencumbered by ancient and archaic eternal truths—can alter society in ways that supposedly modernize and improve it. Furthermore, the individual's focus on self rather than community, and his old habits, beliefs, and traditions, must be altered through socializing education and training, thereby making him the kind of person and citizen whose behavior better conforms to the egalitarian purposes and general welfare of the overall society.

Of course, this is the death of individualism and republicanism. Administrative-state tyranny is precisely the kind of tyranny Alexis de Tocqueville (1805–1859), an iconic French thinker and philosopher, feared for America when he wrote his luminous two-volume book, *Democracy in America*, in 1835 and 1840.[66]

As in the past, I turn to his prescient observations about democracy and America during his travels in this country. Tocqueville wrote, in part: "Nothing is more striking to a European traveler in the United States than the absence of what we term the government, of the administration. Written laws exist in America, and one sees the daily execution of them; but although everything moves regularly, the mover can nowhere be discovered. The hand that directs the social machine is invisible. Nevertheless, as all persons must have recourse to certain grammatical forms, which are the foundation of human language, in order to express their thoughts; so all communities are obliged to secure their existence by submitting to a certain amount of authority, without which they fall into anarchy. . . ."[67] "The administrative power in the United States presents nothing either centralized or hierarchical in its constitution; this accounts for its passing unperceived. The power exists, but its representative is nowhere seen."[68] "In the American republics the central government has never as yet busied itself except with a small number of objects, sufficiently prominent to attract its attention. The secondary affairs of society have never been regulated by its authority; and nothing has hitherto betrayed its desire of even interfering in them. The majority has become more and more absolute, but has not increased the prerogatives of the central government; those great prerogatives have been confined to a certain sphere; and although the despotism of the majority may be galling upon one point, it cannot be said to extend to all."[69]

As if sensing the onset of the American Progressive Era, Tocqueville amplified further: "This point deserves attention; if a democratic republic, similar to that of the United States, were ever founded in a country where the power of one man had previously established a centralized administration and had sunk it deep into the habits and the laws of the people, I do not hesitate to assert that in such a republic a more insufferable despotism would prevail than in any of the absolute monarchies of Europe; or, indeed, than any that could be found on this side of Asia."[70] The despotism of which Tocqueville spoke was of politically misapplied or imposed equality of social and economic conditions (in this he was not rejecting human equality and equal justice, which he vigorously advocated, but the sort of administrative social engineering of the individual and his environment that seeks conformity over individuality). Tocqueville explained: "[T]he vices which despotism produces are precisely those which equality fosters. These two things perniciously complete and assist each other. . . ."[71] "The Americans have combated, by free institutions the tendency of equality to keep men asunder, and they have subdued it. . . . The general affairs of a country engage the attention only of leading politicians, who assemble from time to time in the same places; and as they often lose sight of each other afterwards, no lasting ties are established between them. But if the object be to have the local affairs of a district conducted by the men who reside there, the same persons are always in contact, and they are, in a manner, forced to be acquainted and to adapt themselves to one another." "Thus far more may be done by entrusting to the citizens the administration of minor affairs than by surrendering them in the public welfare and convincing them that they constantly stand in need of one another in order to provide for it. . . . Local freedom, then, which leads a great number of citizens to value the affection of their neighbors and of their kindred, perpetually brings men together and forces them to help one another in spite of the propensities that sever them."[72]

And then Tocqueville warned that "the species of oppression by which democratic nations are menaced is unlike anything that ever before existed in the world; our contemporaries will find no prototype of it in their memories. . . . I have no fear that [the people] will meet tyrants in their rulers, but rather with their guardians."[73] "The first thing that strikes the observation is an innumerable multitude of men, all equal and alike, incessantly endeavoring to procure the petty and paltry pleasures with which they glut their lives. Each of them, living apart, is a stranger to the fate of all the rest; his children and his private friends constitute to him the whole of mankind. As for the rest of his fellow citizens, he is close to them, but he does not see them; he touches them, but he does not feel them; he exists only in himself and for himself alone; and if his kindred still remain to him, he may be said at any rate to have lost his country."[74]

By stripping the individual of his uniqueness and spirit, the democracy transitions into an omnipresent state. "Above this race of men stands an immense and tutelary power, which takes upon itself alone to secure their gratifications and to watch over their fate. That power is absolute, minute, regular, provident, and mild. It would be like the authority of a parent if, like that authority, its object was to prepare men for manhood; but it seeks, on the contrary, to keep them in perpetual childhood: it is well content that the people should rejoice, provided they think nothing but rejoicing. For their happiness such a government willingly labors, but it chooses to be the sole agent and the only arbiter of that happiness; it provides for their security, foresees and supplies their necessities, facilitates their pleasures, manages their principal concerns, directs their industry, regulates the descent of property, and subdivides their inheritances; what remains, but to spare them all the care of thinking and all the trouble of living? Thus it every day renders the exercise of the free agency of man less useful and less frequent; it circumscribes the will within a narrower range and gradually robs a man of all the uses of himself. The principle of equality has prepared men for these things; it has predisposed men to endure them and often to look on them as benefits."[75]

As if describing the progressive's ideological plan, Tocqueville added: "After having thus successively taken each member of the community in its powerful grasp and fashioned him at will, the supreme power then extends its arm over the whole community. It covers the surface of society with a network of small complicated rules, minute and uniform, through which the most original minds and the most energetic characters cannot penetrate, to rise above the crowd. The will of man is not shattered, but softened, bent, and guided; men are seldom forced by it to act, but they are constantly restrained from acting. Such a power does not destroy, but prevents existence; it does not tyrannize, but it compresses, enervates, extinguishes, and stupefies a people, till each nation is reduced to nothing better than a flock of timid and industrious animals, of which the government is the shepherd."[76] Moreover, Tocqueville understood how this form of oppression would be sold to the American people. "I have always thought that servitude of the regular, quiet, and gentle kind which I have just described might be combined more easily than is commonly believed with some of the outward forms of freedom, and that it might even establish itself under the wing of the sovereignty of the people."[77]

What is left, then, is administrative-state tyranny. "Subjection in minor affairs breaks out every day and is felt by the whole community indiscriminately. It does not drive men to resistance, but it crosses them at every turn, till they are led to surrender the exercise of their own will. Thus their spirit is gradually broken and their character enervated; whereas that obedience which is exacted on a few important but rare occasions only exhibits servitude at certain intervals and throws the burden of it upon a small number of men. It is in vain to summon a people who have been rendered so dependent on the central power to choose from time to time the representatives of that power; this rare and brief exercise of their free choice, however important it may be, will not prevent them from gradually losing the faculties of thinking, feeling, and acting for themselves, and thus gradually falling below the level of humanity."[78]

Thus, while claiming to extend true democracy, the people are made subservient to their guardians and the state. "The democratic nations that have introduced freedom into their political constitution at the very time when they were augmenting the despotism of their administrative constitution have been led into strange paradoxes. To manage those minor affairs in which good sense is all that is wanted, the people are held to be unequal to the task; but when the government of the country is at stake, the people are invested with immense powers; they are alternately made the playthings of their ruler, and his masters, more than kings and less than men. . . . It is indeed difficult to conceive how men who have entirely given up the habit of self-government should succeed in making a proper choice of those by whom they are to be governed; and no one will ever believe that a liberal, wise, and energetic government can spring from the suffrages of a subservient people."[79]

THREE

# THE PHILOSOPHER-KINGS

IN *AMERITOPIA*, I WROTE of the philosophers who best describe what I term the utopian mind-set and its application to modern-day utopian thinking and conduct in America, which certainly includes progressivism. I explained that "Plato's *Republic*, Thomas More's *Utopia*, Thomas Hobbes's *Leviathan*, and Karl Marx's *Communist Manifesto* are indispensable in understanding the nature of utopian statism. They are essential works that have in common soulless societies in which the individual is subsumed into a miasma of despotism—and each of them is a warning against utopian transformation in America and elsewhere."[1] But the progressives were also guided by the societal observations and formulations proffered by, among other philosophers, Jean-Jacques Rousseau (1712–1778) and

Georg Wilhelm Friedrich Hegel (1770–1831). Therefore, a partial but useful introduction to their writings is essential, as is another look at Karl Marx (1818–1883).

Jean-Jacques Rousseau was a Swiss-French theorist who had a dreadfully bleak view of the individual and humanity. For Rousseau, societies are built on existing conditions of inequality, competition among individuals breeds exploitation, and the individual is more inclined toward vice than virtue. Therefore, he dismisses natural law and its moral order as a useless jumble, much like his modern progressive descendants. In "Discourse on the Origin of Inequality" (1755), Rousseau asserted:

> Knowing nature so little and agreeing so poorly on the meaning of the word "law," it would be quite difficult to come to some common understanding regarding a good definition of natural law. Thus all those definitions that are found in books have, over and above a lack of uniformity, the added fault of being drawn from several branches of knowledge that men do not naturally have, and from advantages the idea of which they cannot conceive until after having left the state of nature. Writers begin by seeking the rules on which, for the common utility, it would be appropriate for men to agree among themselves; and then they give the name *natural law* to the collection of these rules, with no other proof than the good that presumably would result from their universal

> observance. Surely this is a very convenient way to compose definitions and explain the nature of virtually arbitrary views of what is seemly.[2]

Rousseau also believed that the civil society as constituted was corrupt, had no moral claim, and, in fact, enslaved the individual to existing law and other men. For the most part, the history of society and government was mainly a succession of unequal systems and arrangements, one built atop another, followed by revolution.

Rousseau pointed to two obvious kinds of inequality, the second of which becomes the focus of his academic progeny: "I conceive of two kinds of inequality in the human species: one that I call natural and physical, because it is established by nature and consists in the difference of age, health, bodily strength, and qualities of mind or soul. The other may be called moral or political inequality, because it depends on a kind of convention and is established, or at least authorized, by the consent of men. This latter type of inequality consists in the different privileges enjoyed by some at the expense of others, such as being richer, more honored, more powerful than they, or even causing themselves to be obeyed by them."[3]

This goes to the heart of it. Rousseau's objection was with the nature of humankind. Individuals are different in infinite ways. That has always been and always will be the case. But what binds individuals is exactly what Rousseau criticized. As John Locke put it: "The state of Nature has a law of Nature to govern it, which obliges everyone, and reason, which is that law, teaches all mankind who will but consult it, that being all equal and independent, no one ought to harm another in life, health, liberty or possessions. . . ."[4]

Rousseau elaborated further on life's inequities:

> [I]t is easy to see that, among the differences that distinguish men, several of them pass for natural ones that are exclusively the work of habit and of the various sorts of life that men adopt in society. Thus a robust or delicate temperament, and the strength or weakness that depend on it, frequently derive more from the harsh or effeminate way in which one has been raised than from the primitive constitution of one's body. The same holds for mental powers; and not only does education make a difference between cultivated minds and those that are not, it also augments the difference among the former in proportion to their culture; for were a giant and a dwarf walking on the same road, each step they both took would give a fresh advantage to the giant. Now if one compares the prodigious diversity of educations and lifestyles to be found in the different orders of the civil state with the simplicity and uniformity of animal and savage life, where all nourish themselves from the same foods, live in the same manner, and do exactly the same things, it will be understood how much less the difference

> between one man and another must be in the state of nature than in that society, and how much natural inequality must increase in the human species through inequality occasioned by social institutions. . . .[5]

For Rousseau, where there was private property, economic progress, competition, and wealth creation, there was no escaping economic or social inequality, which he saw as a toxic injustice. It was endemic to the social condition that existed in increasingly complex economies and societies. He wrote: "As long as men were content with the rustic huts, as long as they were limited to making their clothing out of skins sewn together with thorns or fish bones, adorning themselves with feathers and shells, painting their bodies with various colors, perfecting or embellishing their bows and arrows, using sharp-edged stones to make some fishing canoes or some crude musical instruments; in a word, as long as they applied themselves exclusively to tasks that a single individual could do and to the arts that did not require the cooperation of several hands, they lived as free, healthy, good, and happy as they could in accordance with their nature; and they continued to enjoy among themselves the sweet rewards of independent intercourse. But as soon as one man needed the help of another, as soon as one man realized that it was useful for a single individual to have provisions for two, equality disappeared, property came into existence, labor became necessary. Vast forests were transformed into smiling fields that had to be watered with men's sweat, and in which slavery and misery were soon seen to germinate and grow with the crops."[6]

Of course, for America's Founders, equality was not about material equity or social uniformity, truly absurd notions then as now for their impossibility, which should be self-evident, but the principle of unalienable rights for each individual and the impartial application of just laws. Rousseau wrote further: "If we follow the progress of inequality [in the history of governing systems], we will find that the first stage was the establishment of the law and of the right of property, the second stage was the institution of magistracy, and the third and final stage was the transformation of legitimate power into arbitrary power. Thus the condition of rich and poor was authorized by the first epoch, that of the strong and weak by the second, and that of master and slave by the third: the ultimate degree of inequality and the limit to which all the others finally lead, until new revolutions completely dissolve the government or bring it neater to a legitimate institution."[7]

Rousseau then contended that the way around this desolation is for the individual not to focus on his own vanity, needs, wants, etc., but instead to identify with the general will, the public good, and the welfare of society—an egalitarian utopia. Thus individual rights and freedom are renounced and transferred to the collective, where the individual is forced to be free, forming a whole person through the collective. In *Discourse on Political Economy* (1755), Rousseau explained: "The body politic, taken individually, can be considered to be like a body that is organized, living, and similar to that of a man. The sovereign power represents the head; the laws and customs are the brain, source of the nerves, and seat of the understanding, the will, and the senses, of which the judges and magistrates are the organs; the commerce, industry, and agriculture are the mouth and stomach that prepare the common subsistence; the public finances are the blood that is discharged by a wise economy, performing the functions of the heart in order to distribute nourishment and life throughout the body; the citizens are the body and limbs that make the machine move, live, and work and that cannot be harmed in any part without a painful impression immediately being transmitted to the brain, if the animal is in a state of good health. The life of both [the human body and the state] is the *self* common to the whole, the reciprocal sensibility, and the internal coordination of all the parts. What if this communication were to cease, if the formal unity were to disappear, and if contiguous parts were to be related to one another solely by their juxtaposition? The man is dead or the state is dissolved."[8]

Like the recurring theme with modern progressives, Rousseau compared the body politic to the human body, where in order to function as a perfect state, the state must be composed of all the parts of society. Furthermore, the best society is where the individual is at one with the state. Indeed, in his second essential rule of public economy, Rousseau expounded further on what becomes increasingly evident—his prescription for tyranny. "Do you want the general will to be accomplished? Make all private wills be in conformity with it. And since virtue is merely this conformity of the private to the general will, in a word, make virtue reign."[9] The duty of the citizen, then, is above all else to the collective good. And when governing officials are cultivating the collective good, they and the politics of governing are said to be less consequential. "[W]hen citizens love their duty, and when those entrusted with public authority sincerely apply themselves to nurturing this love through their example and efforts, all difficulties vanish and administration takes on an easiness that enables it to dispense with that shady art whose murkiness constitutes its entire mystery. . . . Public mores stand in for the genius of the leaders; and the more virtue reigns the less talents are needed. . . ."[10] Moreover, Rousseau declared: "It is not enough to say to the citizens: be good. They must be taught to be so; and example itself, which is in this respect the first lesson, is not the only means to be used. Love of country is the most effective, for as I have already said, every man is virtuous when his private will is in conformity with the general will in all things, and we willingly want what is wanted by the people we love."[11]

When it comes to government, Rousseau argued that the legislative power belongs to the people but the "supreme administration" or executive, which carries out government administration, does not belong to the people, for its task, albeit important, is nothing more than ministerial. In "Discourse on Social Contract" (1762), Rousseau wrote: "We have seen the legislative power belongs to the people and can belong to it alone. On the contrary . . . executive power cannot belong to the people at large in its role as legislator or sovereign, since this power consists solely of particular acts that are not within the province of the law, nor consequently of the sovereign, none of whose acts can avoid being laws."[12] Rousseau explained that there is a "public force" that "must have an agent of its own that unifies it and gets it working in accordance with the directions of the general will, that serves as a means of communication between the state and the sovereign, and that accomplishes in the public person just about what the union of soul and body accomplishes in man. This is the reason for having government in the state, something often badly confused with the sovereign, of which it is merely the servant."[13]

"What then is government?" asked Rousseau. "An intermediate body established between the subjects and the sovereign for their mutual communication and charged with the execution of the laws and the preservation of liberty, both civil and political."[14] "The government receives from the sovereign the orders it gives the people, and for the state to be in good equilibrium, there must, all things considered, be an equality between the output or the power of the government, taken by itself, and the output or power of the citizens, who are sovereigns on the one hand and subjects on the other."[15]

Rousseau contended that the democratically elected sovereign (the legislature) represents the will of the people, which the unelected executive is compelled to follow. "[T]he trustees of the executive power are not the masters of the populace but its officers; that it can establish and remove them when it pleases. . . ." The trustees simply obey and implement the general will. "[T]hey merely fulfill their duty as citizens, without in any way having the right to dispute over the conditions."[16] However, how is the "general will" discerned? After all, Rousseau asserted that "[t]here is often a great deal of difference between the will of all and the general will. The latter considers only the general interest, whereas the former considers private interest and is merely the sum of private wills. But remove from these same wills the pluses and minuses that cancel each other out, and what remains as the sum of the differences is the general will."[17]

Of course, Rousseau's formulation is incongruous. If the legislature (the sovereign) represents the will of the people, but the will of the people is not necessarily the same as the general will, and if the sole job of the executive (the government) is to institute the decisions of the legislature (the will of the people), then who discerns what the general will is and institutes it? Hence much governing discretion exists in the ambiguity of Rousseau's construct, particularly respecting the executive, even though Rousseau clearly opposed the tyranny of the government. However, he would not reject the totalitarianism of the collective, for it is the manifestation of the general will, which is infallible. In fact, among the adherents to Rousseau's teachings was Maximilien François Marie Isidore de Robespierre (1758–1794), a bloodthirsty leader of the radical Jacobins during the French Revolution's Reign of Terror.

Consequently, Rousseau simultaneously preaches the individual's subordination to society and the illegitimacy of social restraint on the individual. Indeed, because Rousseau rejected precepts of natural law and actual individualism for a socialist mysticism, it follows that he must also reject the governing construct that secures individual free will, ordered liberty, and the moral order—namely, constitutional republicanism. This helps explain the Progressive Era mind-set and approach that followed one hundred years later—that is, arguing for more direct democracy (in the name of "the will of the people") while championing centralized, autocratic rule (in the name of the "general will"), an impossible notion that plagues American society and others to this day.

We are next compelled to turn to German philosopher Georg Wilhelm Friedrich Hegel (1770–1831), whose writings held great sway over not only Marx and Friedrich Engels (1820–1895), but also American progressives, including Croly, Wilson, Dewey, and Weyl. Hegel provided the most detailed exposition of what was known as the period of German idealism. Hegel's influence reaches deep into modern American society. He was a prolific author on many subjects beyond political philosophy; therefore, it will be necessary to limit our scrutiny.

As a starting point, Hegel is legendary for, among other

things, developing the philosophy of historical progress like no other before him. In brief, Hegel argued that he is not inventing a new philosophy but describing the existing reality. The history of the world is said to be progress toward conscious freedom and a state of harmony. Conscious freedom is based on reason and spiritual principles (meaning self-realization), as opposed to social customs, rituals, and habits, which subordinate the individual's intellect, reasoning, and reflection. Hegel argued that human development, or the lack thereof, changes from one historical period to the next. Some societies are stuck in their own history, and others progress over time, but the trajectory of history generally is toward the ideal state. The method of individual and societal progress involves a dialectic process—some reasoned, some unconscious—in which opposites are in a constant state of conflict, synthesizing into ever-higher truths, which eventually lead to a fully developed state—the "final end." That which appears irrational in a state will eventually be brought into harmony. And this, contended Hegel, is the fact of human history and evolution.

Furthermore, the state is ultimately the external force (as opposed to eternal force) through which the individual finds his actualization—liberty, happiness, and fulfillment. As such, the individual is not consumed with his own existence and private affairs ("subjective thought"). Rather, by way of the state, the individual sees beyond self and becomes a citizen of the state, whose reality is part of a universalized whole and collective life, through which the individual learns what is reasonable ("objective thought"). This is the final end sought by the individual and the state—the consciousness of mind and freedom. In this way, the individual serves and benefits from the state and vice versa. That which came before effectively vanishes. Therefore, man progressively moves away from the state of nature to the final end through reason.

In *Elements of the Philosophy of Right* (1820), Hegel wrote of the ideal state thus: "The state is the realized ethical idea or ethical spirit. It is the will which manifests itself, makes itself clear and visible, substantiates itself. It is the will which thinks and knows. The state finds in ethical custom its direct and unreflected existence, and its indirect and reflected existence in the self-consciousness of the individual and in his knowledge and activity. Self-consciousness in the form of social disposition has its substantive freedom in the state, as the essence, purpose, and product of its activity. . . . The state, which is the realized substantive will, having its reality in the particular self-consciousness raised to the plane of the universal, is absolutely rational. This substantive unity is its own motive and absolute end. In this end freedom attains its highest right. This end has the highest right over the individual, whose highest duty in turn is to be a member of the state."[18]

Therefore, the individual is again subservient to the state, for the state can never attain the lofty utopian heights devised by Hegel, and the individual will never be adequate to the cause. Meanwhile, the individual's independence and free will are absorbed by the state in the name of community and general welfare. Indeed, the unity of the "actualized" individual with the ideal state requires the abandonment of the past. Hegel found no relevance at all in the origin and founding principles of a nation, except to understand the next step in the historical process and the synthesizing that comes from dialecticism. In fact, Hegel took a direct shot at the notion of eternal natural law and rights, as well as the social contract, which, of course, are the bases of America's founding and the Declaration of Independence. He insisted that the only legitimate form of thought involves the application of "the science of the state." Sound familiar? This is a constant theme among American progressives—the diminution of the individual and the rejection of America's heritage. Hegel went on: "Rationality, viewed abstractly, consists in the thorough unity of universality and individuality. Taken concretely, and from the standpoint of the content, it is the unity of objective freedom with the subjective freedom, of the general substantive will with the individual consciousness and the individual will seeking particular ends. From the standpoint of the form it consists in action determined by thought-out or universal laws and principles.—This idea of the state is not concerned with the historical origin of either the state in general or of any particular state with its special rights and characters. Hence, it is indifferent whether the state arose out of the patriarchal condition, out of fear or confidence, or out of the corporation. It does not care whether the basis of state rights is declared to be in the divine, or in a positive right, or contract, or custom.

When we are dealing simply with the science of the state, these things are mere appearances, and belong to history. The causes or grounds of the authority of an actual state, in so far as they are required at all, must be derived from the forms of right, which have validity in the state."[19]

Of course, Hegel found no perfect state, for none has ever existed, not then or before. But there are positives that exist in every state, and it is these positives that are the building blocks to the next level and, eventually, to the final end. Hegel explained: "The state as a completed reality is the ethical whole and the actualization of freedom. It is the absolute purpose of reason that freedom should be actualized. The state is the spirit, which abides in the world and there realizes itself consciously; while in nature it is realized only as the other of itself or the sleeping spirit. Only when it is present in consciousness, knowing itself as an existing object, is it the state. In thinking of freedom we must not take our departure from individuality or the individual's self-consciousness, but from the essence of self-consciousness. Let man be aware of it or not, this essence realizes itself as an independent power, in which particular persons are only phases. The state is the march of God in the world; its ground or cause is the power of reason realizing itself as will. When thinking of the idea of the state, we must not have in mind any particular state, or particular institution, but must rather contemplate the idea, this actual God, by itself. Although the state may be declared to violate right principles and to be defective in various ways, it always contains the essential elements of its existence, if, that is to say, it belongs to the full formed state of our own time. But as it is more easy to detect short-comings than to grasp the positive meaning, one easily falls into the mistake of dwelling so much upon special aspects of the state as to overlook its inner organic being. The state is not a work of art. It is in the world, in the sphere of caprice, accident, and error. Evil behavior can doubtless disfigure it in many ways, but the ugliest man, the criminal, the invalid, the cripple, are living men. The positive thing, the life, is present in spite of defects, and it is with this affirmative that we have here to deal."[20]

Time and again, Hegel described the dialectic of opposites posed against one another as a productive process that leads to the actualized person and state. He further illustrated this point by also comparing the state to a living organism. "Political disposition is given definite content by the different phases of the organism of the state. This organism is the development of the idea into its differences, which are objectively actualized. These differences are the different functions, affairs, and activities of state. By means of them the universal uninterruptedly produces itself, by a process which is a necessary one, since these various offices proceed from the nature of conception."[21] "The state is an organism or the development of the idea into its differences. These different sides are the different functions, affairs and activities of state by means of which the universal unceasingly produces itself by a necessary process. At the same time it is self-contained, since it is presupposed in its own productive activity. This organism is the political constitution. It proceeds eternally out of the state, just as the state in turn is self-contained by means of the constitution. If these two things fall apart, and make the different aspects independent, the unity produced by the constitution is no longer established. The true relation is illustrated by the fable of the belly and the limbs. Although the parts of an organism do not constitute an identity, yet it is of such a nature that, if one of its parts makes itself independent, all must be harmed. . . ."[22] "The idealism, which constitutes sovereignty, is that point of view in accordance with which the so-called parts of an animal organism are not parts but members of organic elements. Their isolation or independent subsistence would be a disease. . . ."[23]

Given Hegel's philosophy of history and historical progress, and the incompleteness of one historical period to the next, clearly no state has reached such a status and, in reality, no state ever will. Therefore, while preaching that his thinking is not about creating a philosophy but understanding reality, is not Hegel doing both, including inventing the ultimate abstraction—the "final end"? Indeed, up to this point his argument leads to fundamental ambiguities, which raise several questions. For example, how is the individual or the citizenry to know when society has reached the final end? How is this decided? Who decides? And if the final end has been reached, then what? Heaven on earth? Furthermore, is the individual to abandon his "subjective thought" and, therefore, his actual individuality, for the "objective thought" of a flawed or imperfect state that has not reached the final end? Yet how is the final end to be achieved if the individual does not submit to the collective subjective thought in advance of the final end—that is, must he submit to a pre–final end state? And if he does, how does becoming at one with such a flawed or imperfect state contribute to productive historical synthesizing and lead to harmony when it will likely lead to the opposite—the perpetuation of a flawed or imperfect state?

In his book *The Open Society and Its Enemies* (1945), Karl Popper (1902–1994), an Austrian-British philosopher and strong Hegel critic, exposed Hegel's illogic: "Hegel's intention is to operate freely with all contradictions. 'All things are contradictory in themselves,' he insists, in order to defend a position which means the end not only of all science, but of all rational argument. And the reason why he wishes to admit contradictions is that he wants to stop rational argument, and with it scientific and intellectual progress. By making argument and criticism impossible, he intends to make his own philosophy proof against all criticism, so that it may establish itself as a *reinforced dogmatism*, secure from every attack, and the insurmountable summit of all philosophical development."[24]

Hegel proved Popper's position when he, among other things, disparaged natural law, external truths, divine rights, etc., as fundamentally mythological and superficial. "Concerning [a] constitution, as concerning reason itself, there has in modern times been an endless babble, which has in Germany been more insipid than anywhere else. With us there are those who have persuaded themselves that it is best even at the very threshold of government to understand before all other things what a constitution is. And they think that they have furnished invincible proof that religion and piety should be the basis of all their shallowness. It is small wonder if this prating has made for reasonable mortals the words reason, illumination, right, constitution, liberty, mere empty sounds, and men should have become ashamed to talk about political constitution. At least as one effect of this superfluity, we may hope to see the conviction becoming general, that a philosophic acquaintance with such topics cannot proceed from mere reasons, ends, grounds, and utilities, much less from feeling, love, and inspiration, but only out of the conception. It will be a fortunate thing, too, if those who maintain the divine to be inconceivable and an acquaintance with the truth to be wasted effort, were henceforth to refrain from breaking in upon the argument. What of undigested rhetoric and edification they manufacture out of these feelings can at least lay no claim to philosophic notice."[25]

Hegel then denounced the doctrine of separation of powers, the purpose of which is to contain the power of the state and protect the individual from the tyranny that typically arises from the centralization of power. "Amongst current ideas must be mentioned . . . that regarding the necessary division of the functions of the state. This is a most important feature, which, when taken in its true sense, is rightly regarded as the guarantee of public freedom. But of this those, who think to speak out of inspiration and love, neither know nor will know anything, for in it lies the element of determination through the way of reason. The principle of the separation of functions contains the essential element of difference, that is to say, of rationality. But as apprehended by the abstract understanding it is false when it leads to the view that these several functions are absolutely independent, and it is one-sided when it considers the relation of these functions to one another as negative and mutually limiting. In such a view each function in hostility to or fear of the others acts towards them as towards an evil. Each resolves to oppose the others, effecting by this opposition of forces a general balance, it may be, but not a living unity. . . . To take the negative as the point of departure, and set up as primary the willing of evil and consequent mistrust, and then on this supposition cunningly to devise breakwaters, which in turn require other breakwaters to check their activity, any such contrivance is the mark of a thought, which is at the level of the negative understanding, and of a feeling, which is characteristic of the rabble. . . ."[26]

Consequently, despite his extensive argument about conscious freedom (reason and spirituality), a community of the whole (egalitarianism), the ambiguity of the practical form of the final end (the eventual perfect state), and the condemnation of constitutional republicanism (as disparate parts of the

same organ devouring itself), Hegel finally revealed himself as a monarchist. "The legislative corresponds to universality, and the executive to particularity; but the judicial is not the third element of the conception. The individuality uniting the other two lies beyond these spheres. . . . The function of the prince, as the subjectivity with which rests the final decision. In this function the other two are brought into an individual unity. It is at once the culmination and beginning of the whole. This is constitutional monarchy."[27] Hence Hegel's final end is an all-knowing, all-powerful monarchy. "The perfecting of the state into a constitutional monarchy is the work of the modern world, in which the substantive idea has attained the infinite form. This is the descent of the spirit of the world into itself, the free perfection by virtue of which the idea sets loose from itself its own elements, and nothing but its own elements, and makes them totalities . . ."[28]

To the critics of monarchy, Hegel wrote: "The conception of monarch offers great difficulty to abstract reasoning and to the reflective methods of the understanding. The understanding never gets beyond isolated determinations, and ascribes merit to mere reasons, or finite points of view and what can be derived from them. Thus the dignity of the monarch is represented as something derivative not only in its form but also in its essential character. . . . If by the phrase 'sovereignty of the people' is to be understood a republic, or more precisely a democracy, all that is necessary has already been said." Hegel is talking about his previous denunciation of separation of pow-

ers, etc. In defense of monarchy Hegel added: "When a people is not a patriarchal tribe, having passed from the primitive condition, which made the forms of aristocracy and democracy possible, and is represented not as in a willful and unorganized condition, but as a self-developed truly organic totality, in such a people sovereignty is the personality of the whole, and exists, too, in a reality, which is proportionate to the conception, the person of the monarch."[29]

Popper saw the danger inherent in Hegel's historic dialectic: "I have tried to show the identity of Hegelian historicism with the philosophy of modern totalitarianism. This identity is seldom clearly enough realized. Hegelian historicism has become the language of wide circles of intellectuals, even of the candid 'anti-fascists' and 'leftist.' It is so much a part of their intellectual atmosphere that, for many, it is no more noticeable, and its appalling dishonesty no more remarkable, than the air they breathe." Popper went on: "The Hegelian farce has done enough harm. We must stop it." Condemning the intellectuals and teachers who ignore the warnings about Hegel's thinking, Popper declared that "they neglected them not so much at their own peril (they did not fare badly) as at the peril of those whom they taught, and at the peril of mankind."[30]

This brings us unavoidably to a concise examination of Karl Marx, since his effect on American progressivism, among other intellectual and political movements in other societies, is undeniable. Marx, who was also a German philosopher, carefully studied Hegel's writings, as did his frequent

partner, Friedrich Engels. "Marxism's" intellectual starting point is nearly indistinguishable from Hegel's. Marx also saw history as the past and the present washed away through the perfecting of society. However, Marx argued that Hegel's idealistic historicism, and its emphasis on legal and political conditions, failed to account sufficiently for the most important characteristic of historical progress—economics. Marx insisted that economics is the key to society and life, or what would be defined as material historicism or dialectical materialism. Mankind starts with needs, which evolve into conscious production; Marx contended that man is not about the natural individual, the rational individual, or the political life but rather man as he exists, thereby attempting to distinguish his own philosophy from, say, Rousseau, Hegel, and others. Marx asserted that man's life revolves around labor and production, and conditions external to himself, to which he must adapt. Thus the conditions of production determine economic relations, and history shows that these economic relations have been about class struggle.

In *The Communist Manifesto* (1848), Marx wrote about material historicism accordingly: "All property relations in the past have continually been subject to historical change, consequent upon the change of historical conditions."[31] More specifically, "[t]he history of all hitherto existing society is the history of class struggles. Freeman and slave, patrician and plebeian, lord and serf, guild master and journeyman, in a word, oppressor and oppressed, stood in constant opposition to one another, carried on an uninterrupted, now hidden, open fight, that each time ended, either in the revolutionary reconstitution of society at large, or in the common ruin of the contending classes. In earlier epochs of history we find almost everywhere a complicated arrangement of society into various orders, manifold gradation of social rank. In ancient Rome we have patricians, knights, plebeians, slaves; in the middle ages, feudal lords, vassals, guild masters, journeymen, apprentices, serfs; in almost all these classes, again, subordinate gradations."[32] Thus Marx's focus on the "division of labor," the "fragmentation of productive forces," and the "mode of production" of the "species-being" known as human beings. Along with private property rights, he claimed that they create alienation and the artificial sense of individual purpose and private existence.

Let me suggest, however, that the history of man and his struggles is diverse and mixed, well beyond materialism and economics. Struggles within societies, struggles between societies, struggles among and between groups of individuals in societies, and struggles between individuals in societies may be based on race, religion, tribalism, mysticism, geography, or wealth, or some combination of factors, including those that may not be known to or understood by contemporary man. They are rational and irrational, intentional and accidental, historic and modern. Furthermore, all of life is not about struggles among and between people or forced associations, economic or otherwise. Individuals can choose their own fate; they can choose to associate with whom they wish and in a variety of ways, unrelated to production, materialism, or satisfying their own economic needs.

Nonetheless, Marx wrote, "The modern bourgeois society that has sprouted from the ruins of feudal society has not done away with class antagonism. It has but established new classes, new conditions of oppression, new forms of struggle in place of the old ones. Our epoch, the epoch of the bourgeois, possesses, however, this distinctive feature; it has simplified the class antagonisms. Society as a whole is more and more splitting up into two great hostile camps, into two great classes directly facing each other: Bourgeoisie [the capitalists, the owners of property and the means of production] and Proletariat [the laborer, the industrial working class] . . . Modern industry has established the world's market, for which the discovery of America paved the way. The market has given an immense development to commerce, to navigation, to communication by land. This development has, in its turn, reacted on the extension of industry; and in proportion as industry, commerce, navigation and railways extended, in the same proportion the bourgeoisie developed, increased its capital, and pushed into the background every class handed down from the Middle Ages. We see, therefore, how the modern bourgeoisie is itself the product of a long course of development, of a series of revolutions in the modes of production and of exchange."[33]

Marx asserted that it is the bourgeoisie that benefits greatly from the status quo, and the proletariat that suffers from it. "The bourgeoisie, wherever it has got the upper hand, has put an end to all feudal, patriarchal, idyllic relations. It has pitilessly torn asunder the motley feudal ties that bound man to his 'natural superiors,' and has left remaining no other nexus between man and man than naked self-interest, callous 'cash payment.' It has drowned the most heavenly ecstasies of religious fervor, of chivalrous enthusiasm, of philistine sentimentalism, in the icy water of egotistical calculation. It has resolved personal worth into exchange value, and in place of the numberless indefeasible chartered freedoms, has set up that single, unconscionable freedom—Free Trade. In one word, for exploitation, veiled by religious and political illusions, it has substituted naked, shameless, brutal exploitation. The bourgeoisie has stripped of its halo every occupation hitherto honored and looked up to with reverent awe. It has converted the physician, the lawyer, the priest, the poet, the man of science, into its paid wage laborers. The bourgeoisie has torn away from the family its sentimental veil, and has reduced the family relation to a mere money relation."[34]

Moreover, wrote Marx, the bourgeoisie must continually expand its holdings and reach, all the time exploiting the labor of the proletariat to enrich itself. "The bourgeoisie cannot exist without constantly revolutionizing the instruments of production, and thereby the relations of production, and with them the whole relations of society. . . . Constant revolutionizing of production, uninterrupted disturbance of all social conditions, everlasting uncertainty and agitation, distinguish the bourgeoisie epoch from all earlier ones. . . . The need of a constantly expanding market for its products chases the bourgeoisie over the whole surface of the globe. It must nestle everywhere, settle everywhere, establish connections everywhere."[35] Consequently, capitalism replaces feudalism, the former even more reprehensible in Marx's eyes than the latter. Feudalism's productive forces were "burst asunder" and "[i]nto their place stepped free competition, accompanied by a social and political constitution adapted to it, and by the economical and political sway of the bourgeois class. A similar movement is going on before our own eyes. Modern bourgeois society with its relations of production, of exchange, and of property, a society that has conjured up such gigantic means of production and of exchange, is like the sorcerer, who is no longer able to control the powers of the nether world whom he has called up by his spells."[36]

For the proletariat, there is no escaping the bourgeois state as it covers and controls all corners of the society. "In proportion as the bourgeoisie, i.e., capital, is developed, in the same proportion is the proletariat, the modern working class, developed; a class of laborers, who live only so long as they find work, and who find work only so long as their labor increases capital. These laborers, who must sell themselves piecemeal, are a commodity, like every other article of commerce, and are consequently exposed to all the vicissitudes of competition, to all the fluctuations of the market. . . . Modern industry has converted the little workshop of the patriarchal master into the great factory of the industrial capitalist. Masses of laborers, crowded into the factory, are organized like soldiers. As privates of the industrial army they are placed under the command of a perfect hierarchy of officers and sergeants. Not only are they slaves of the bourgeois class, and of the bourgeois State, they are daily and hourly enslaved by the machine, by the over-seer, and, above all, by the individual bourgeois manufacturer himself. The more openly this despotism proclaims gain to be its end and aim, the more petty, the more hateful and the more embittering it is. . . . No sooner is the exploitation of the laborer by the manufacturer so far at an end that he receives his wages in cash, than he is set upon by the other portions of the bourgeoisie; the landlord, the shopkeeper, the pawnbroker, etc."[37]

Consequently, the property owner, businessman, landlord, etc., are cast as the evil, cold-blooded, plundering taskmasters, and the employee and laborer are portrayed as noble, compassionate, powerless, abused, etc. Of course, human beings are not so easily assigned to such ranks and classes by such preconceived and stereotypical characteristics. In fact, most "proletariats" do not feel terrorized by the "bourgeoisie" and therefore do not spontaneously rise to the revolutionary cause; also, most bourgeoisies are not terrorizing their employees or tenants. On the contrary; industrial society is not inherently wicked. It has improved the standard of living for most of the population in a complex society—"bourgeoisie" and "proletariat" alike—where the comforts of a developed economy are available to virtually all who participate in it.

Indeed, the entire nomenclature and class identification devised by Marx is terribly flawed. For example, is there a monolithic, alienated class of workers, or proletariat? French philosopher and journalist Raymond Aron (1905–1983), in his book *The Opium of the Intellectuals* (1955), wrote of the myth of the proletariat: "Why is it so often considered difficult to define the working class? No definition can trace precisely the limits of a category. At what stage in the hierarchy does the skilled worker cease to belong to the proletariat? Is the manual worker in the public services a proletarian even though he receives his wages from the State and not from a private employer? Do the wage-earners in commerce, whose hands manipulate the objects manufactured by others, belong to the same groups as the wage-earners in industry? There can be no dogmatic answer to such queries: they have no common criterion. According to whether one considered the nature of the work, the method and the amount of the remuneration, the style of life, one will or will not include certain workers in the category of proletarians. The garage mechanic, a wage-earning manual worker, is in a different position and has a different outlook on society from the worker employed on an assembly-line in a motor-car factory. . . ."[38]

Aron illuminated further: "The contempt with which the intellectuals are inclined to regard everything connected with commerce and industry has always seemed to me itself contemptible. That the same people who look down on engineers or industrialists profess to recognize universal man in the worker at his lathe or on the assembly line, seems to me endearing but somewhat surprising. Neither the division of labor nor the raising of the standard of living contributes towards this universalism. . . . Philosophers have the right to hope that the proletarian will not become integrated with the existing order but that he will preserve himself for revolutionary action; but they cannot [in modern times] represent as fact the universality of the industrial worker."[39] "Not all proletarians have the feeling of being exploited or oppressed."[40] "In countries where the economy continues to expand, where the standard of living has risen, why should the real liberties of the proletariat, however partial, be sacrificed to a total liberation which turns out to be indistinguishable from the omnipotence of the State?"[41]

For Marx, the existing institutions have been set up by the ruling class. Therefore, society exists not as a matter of just law, but at the will of the bourgeoisie. The law is nothing more than the means by which the bourgeoisie satisfies its own interests and happiness—that is, the control of production, economic domination, and private property. "All property relations in the past have continually been subject to historical change, consequent upon the change in historical conditions. . . . In this sense the theory of the Communists may be summed up in the single sentence: Abolition of private property."[42] Then, like Rousseau and Hegel before him, and the progressives decades later, Marx attacked natural law and the principles of individual liberty: "The selfish misconception that induces you to transform into eternal laws of nature and of reason, the social forms springing from your present mode of production and form of property—historical relations that rise and disappear in the progress of production—the misconception you share with every ruling class that has preceded you. What you see clearly in the case of ancient property, what you admit in the case of feudal property, you are of course forbidden to admit in the case of your own bourgeois form of property."[43]

Marx also targeted education, for it promotes the status quo; it is only useful if applied as a tool for social justice, a view largely adopted by American intellectuals and educators during the Progressive Era. "And your education! Is not that also social, and determined by social conditions under which you educate, by the intervention, direct or indirect, of society by means of schools, etc.? The Communists have not invented the intervention of society in education; they do but seek to alter the character of that intervention, and to rescue education from the influence of the ruling class."[44]

Marx's goal was not to build on the past or the present,

but to break absolutely from them. "The history of all past society has consisted in the development of class antagonisms, antagonisms that assumed different forms at different epochs. But whatever form they may have taken, one fact is common to all past ages . . . the exploitation of one part of society by the other. No wonder, then, that the social consciousness of past ages, despite all the multiplicity and variety it displays, moves within certain common forms, or general ideas, which cannot completely vanish except with the total disappearance of class antagonisms. The Communist revolution is the most radical rupture with traditional property relations; no wonder that its development involves the most radical rupture with traditional ideas."[45] And the manner in which this revolution and thorough transformation will occur? "The proletariat will use its political supremacy to wrest, by degrees, all capital from the bourgeoisie; to centralize all instruments of production in the hands of the State, i.e., of the proletariat organized as the ruling class; and to increase the total of productive forces as rapidly as possible. Of course, in the beginning this cannot be effected except by means of despotic inroads on the rights of property and on the conditions of the bourgeois production; by means of measures, therefore, which appear economically insufficient and untenable, but which, in the course of the movement, outstrip themselves, necessitate further inroads upon the old social order and are unavoidable as a means of entirely revolutionizing the mode of production."[46]

Therefore, by violence and force, at least at the start, economics, party, politics, and law will all become centralized within the state, until the perfect egalitarian society is established and the individual is emancipated from the productive process, at which point the state itself will wither away. "When, in the course of development, class distinctions have disappeared and all production has been concentrated in the hands of the vast association of the whole nation, the public power will lose its political character. Political power, properly so-called, is merely the organized power of one class for oppressing another. If the proletariat during its contest with the bourgeoisie is compelled, by the force of circumstances, to organize itself as a class, if, by means of revolution, it makes itself the ruling class, and, as such, sweeps away by force the old conditions of production then it will, along with these conditions, have swept away the conditions for the existence of class antagonisms, and of classes generally, and will thereby have abolished its own supremacy as a class."[47]

Popper rightly condemned Marx as a false prophet. "He was a prophet of the course of history, and his prophecies did not come true; but this is not my main accusation. It is much more important that he misled scores of intelligent people into believing that historical prophecy is the scientific way of approaching social problems. . . . Socialism was to be developed from its Utopian stage to its scientific stage; it was to be based upon the scientific method of analyzing cause and effect, and upon scientific prediction. And since he assumed prediction in the field of society to be the same as historical prophecy, scientific socialism was to be based upon a study of the historical causes and historical effect, and finally upon the prophecy of its own advent."[48] "There is no reason why we should believe that, of all sciences, social science is capable of realizing the age-old dream of revealing what the future has in store for us. . . ."[49] This is a spectacular understatement. Between 85 *million and 100 million deaths* are attributed to communism's workers' paradise. And there are the infinite horror stories in places like the People's Republic of China, the former Soviet Union, North Korea, Cuba, Venezuela, and Zimbabwe.[50]

Nonetheless, out of these monumentally flawed theories of human behavior and political organization, and the misinterpretation and misapplication of human history, was born the American progressive movement, the modern forms of which plague the civil society and imperil its existence.

FOUR

# ADMINISTRATIVE-STATE TYRANNY

OBVIOUSLY, AS ONE WOULD expect, there is not a seamless symmetry among and between the various American progressives and certain of the principal philosophers who influenced them. However, there certainly are significant similarities of outlook and attitude toward mankind, economics, law, politics, and government; there is a zealous belief and commitment in reengineering both man's nature and his social environment toward egalitarian and utopian ends; and there is an affinity for centralized rule, whether of the fascistic or socialistic kind, some hybrid thereof, or some derivative thereof. For these reasons and others, the American progressive philosophers, intellectuals, and politicians uniformly disparaged the principles of the American founding, the American civil society, and the American constitutional system. Whether idealistic historicism, material historicism, historic dialecticism, material dialecticism, synthesizing of opposites, actualizing individualism, conscious individualism, egalitarianism, the social sciences, the behavioral sciences, etc., the individual is swept up into, and ultimately disfigured by, a whirlwind of ideological concepts and impossibilities. As the oppressiveness and impracticability of progressivism spreads, the more hard-line and belligerent become its proponents and enforcers. Ultimately, it leads to the unraveling of the civil society.

What is the civil society and why is it so important? As I explained in *Liberty and Tyranny*:

> In the civil society, the *individual* is recognized and accepted as more than an abstract statistic or faceless member of some group; rather, he is a *unique*, *spiritual being* with a soul and a conscience. He is free to discover his own potential and pursue his own legitimate interests, tempered, however, by a *moral order* that has its foundation in *faith* and guides his life and all human life through the *prudent* exercise of judgment. As such, the individual in the civil society strives, albeit imperfectly, to be virtuous—that is, restrained, ethical, and honorable. He rejects the relativism that blurs the lines between good and bad, right and wrong, just and unjust, and means and ends.
>
> In the civil society, the individual has a duty to respect the unalienable rights of others and the values,

customs, and traditions, tried and tested over time and passed from one generation to the next, that establish a society's *cultural identity*. He is responsible for attending to his own well-being and that of his family. And he has a duty as a *citizen* to contribute voluntarily to the welfare of his community through good works.

In the civil society, *private property* and liberty are inseparable. The individual's right to live freely and safely and pursue happiness includes the right to acquire and possess property, which represents the fruits of his own intellectual and/or physical labor. As the individual's time on earth is finite, so, too, is his labor. The illegitimate denial or diminution of his private property enslaves him to another and denies him his liberty.

In the civil society, a *rule of law*, which is just, known, and predictable, and applied equally albeit imperfectly, provides the governing framework for the restraints on the polity, thereby nurturing the civil society and serving as a check against the arbitrary use and, hence, abuse of power.[1]

The civil society predates the constitutional order. Its subjugation and transformation by a voracious and an unappeasable administrative state is the true object of the progressive ideologue. But the purpose of a constitution, or at least the American constitution, is to secure politically the human harmony within the civil society so that individual liberty, equal justice, and the civil order may be nurtured and maintained. The difficulty, as James Madison explained in *Federalist* 51, is to bring order to liberty and liberty to order: "But what is government itself, but the greatest of all reflections on human nature? If men were angels, no government would be necessary. If angels were to govern men, neither external nor internal controls on government would be necessary. In framing a government which is to be administered by men over men, the great difficulty lies in this: you must first enable the government to control the governed; and in the next place oblige it to control itself."[2]

In the Declaration of Independence, the Founders proclaimed "[t]hat to secure these [unalienable] rights [to life, liberty, and the pursuit of happiness], Governments are instituted among Men, deriving their just powers from the consent of the governed. . . ." They went on to say what was intolerable. "That whenever any Form of Government becomes destructive of these ends, it is the Right of the People to alter or to abolish it, and to institute new Government, laying its foundation on such principles and organizing its powers in such form, as to them shall seem most likely to effect their Safety and Happiness." However, the Founders were also fearful of the dangers of constant rebellion and revolution. They made clear that changing governments is a matter of the utmost seriousness, requiring wise judgment. "Prudence, indeed, will dictate that Governments long established should not be changed for light and transient causes; and accordingly all experience hath shewn, that mankind are more disposed to suffer, while evils are sufferable, than to right themselves by abolishing the forms to which they are accustomed. . . ."[3]

Of course, the progressives are well aware that the Declaration, and its governing expression, the Constitution, are enormous impediments to their purposes inasmuch as the form of government that best reflects the values of the civil society and secures its existence is constitutional republicanism. Thus, as is now obvious, various doctrines of administrative-state centralization have been developed and increasingly accepted, where the equivalent of Plato's Guardians (whom I discussed at length in *Ameritopia*)—that is, a select few of highly educated and specially trained governing elite—oversee the operation of society. Progressives insist this is the normal evolution of government from a pioneering, revolutionary period to an increasingly complex and modern society.

However, despite the extensive writings about the supposed professional governing class with specialized expertise that will presumably bring not just order to chaos but utopian-like perfection to humanity, it is fair to ask: Who are these guardians? What makes them experts? Are they experts by specific, technical training or as generalists? Are they experts by graduating from Ivy League schools? Are they experts by experience, knowledge, or judgment? Are they experts by training in the social and behavioral sciences or the physical sciences? Are they experts because they are more humane and compassionate than the citizenry over whom they rule? By what measures or standards are they experts? And who determines that these guardians are experts? Indeed, what makes them more expert, and all that may or may not entail, than those who operate in the private sector? Are the latter not the true experts by experience, training, and knowledge? Moreover, how are their supposed areas of expertise matched with their assignments to particular governmental departments and jobs to ensure the most efficient and effective performance? Are job placements based solely on expertise or other factors, including office politics? In fact, is not the purpose of the civil service and public-sector unionization, and intervening policies such as seniority, affirmative action, tenure, etc., unrelated to or at least potentially contradictory of a purely merit- and expertise-based administrative system?

Furthermore, which decisions are to be left to the private sector? Which decisions are better made in government field offices versus centralized offices? How can centrally located personnel know the conditions, problems, interests, and well-being of local communities, let alone local businesses and individuals? Is there such a thing as excessive centralization? And does it not result in delayed decision making and decisions based on a lack of information and a lack of knowledge? And what is the overarching mission of the experts in the governing class? Is it to follow orders in a mechanical fashion, or the broad discretion to formulate policies? Is it to administratively institute congressional legislation or to micromanage society? Is it to determine the general welfare, public good, and common destiny of America?

How does the voter and the political environment factor into administrative decision making? Do the administrative-state experts even attempt to discern the public will, in particular or general matters, when fashioning rules and regulations? Or do they deem their function apolitical and therefore immune from any such considerations? Indeed, is their purpose to defy the electorate if they perceive the electorate defiant of their expertly determined policy goals? Is it not the case that at the end of every presidential term, the executive branch issues scores if not hundreds of so-called midnight regulations, the purpose of which is to enshrine certain policies of the outgoing administration *after* the voters have exercised their will and *before* the inauguration of the incoming executive? In fact, has not administrative rule substituted for self-governance?

The issues surrounding the centralized administrative state are endless. The progressives and their philosopher-kings, who have debated among themselves for decades and even centuries about the best forms of paradisiacal rule, give scant coherent or practical direction. The fact is that the progressives are no more capable of organizing a complex society than a complex society is capable of being organized.

F. A. Hayek (1899–1992), a luminous philosopher of politics and economics, explained in *The Fatal Conceit* (1988) that progressive intellectuals "appoint themselves as representatives of modern thought, as persons superior in knowledge and moral virtue to any who retain a high regard for traditional values, as persons whose very duty it is to offer new ideas to the public—and who must, in order to make their wares seem novel, deride whatever is conventional. For such people, due to the positions in which they find themselves, 'newness,' or 'news,' and not truth becomes the main value, although that is hardly their intention—and although what they offer is often no more new than it is true. . . ."[4] "[I]ntelligent people will tend to overvalue intelligence, and to suppose that we must owe all the advantages and opportunities that our civilization offers to deliberate design rather than to follow traditional rules, and likewise to suppose that we can, by exercising our reason, eliminate any remaining undesired features by still more intelligent reflection, and still more appropriate design and 'rational coordination' of our undertakings. This leads one to be favorably disposed to [central planning]. . . . [T]hey also understandably will want to align themselves with [administrative] science and reason, and with the extraordinary progress made by the physical sciences during the past several centuries, and since they have been taught that constructivism and scientism are what science and the use of reason are all about, they find it hard to believe that there can exist any useful knowledge that did not originate in deliberate experimentation, or to accept the validity of any tradition apart from their own tradition of reason."[5] Indeed, in *The Constitution of Liberty* (1960), Hayek summed it up this way: "All political theories assume, of course, that most individuals are very ignorant. Those who plead for liberty differ from the rest in that they include among the ignorant themselves as well as the wisest. Compared with the totality of knowledge which is continually utilized in the evolution of a dynamic civilization, the difference between the knowledge that the wisest and that the most ignorant individual can deliberately employ is comparatively insignificant."[6]

In fact, the theology of administrative science and historicism, after more than a century of progressive centralized governance in America, has demonstrated in infinite ways that it is not a science at all. The massive present-day administrative state is inflicted with extensive imperfections and dislocations. Its widespread shortcomings and deficiencies include enormous levels of waste, fraud, and abuse; extensive managerial incompetence and delinquencies; overlapping programs and red tape; and failed promises and objectives—all of which are documented in countless investigations, audits, reports, and books (including my own book *Plunder and Deceit*).[7] There is simply no validation of a vast, complex, modern society humanely and effectively managed by a centralized Leviathan reporting to a single chief executive, the president.

For example, while progressives point to popular entitlement programs such as Social Security and Medicare as models of accomplishment, even these programs have been so badly administered and politicized over the years—including emptying the trusts and individual accounts of their funds and diverting them for general governmental operations, a continuing colossal theft that ensures the programs' bankruptcy in the near future—they have been turned into the equivalent of Ponzi schemes.[8] Therefore, while popular and beneficial to many today, their eventual collapse will be devastating to society and the economy. Other examples abound. The progressives' interference with the housing market through the Community Reinvestment Act resulted in the collapse of that market, a calamitous disaster for millions of homeowners who lost the equity in their homes or lost their homes outright.[9] And the progressives' most recent project, the so-called Patient Protection and Affordable Care Act, or Obamacare, has made health care unaffordable for untold numbers of citizens, driving up the cost of health insurance policies as well as the amount of deductibles and out-of-pocket expenses.[10] Even in the field of education, progressive policies have driven up the costs at every stage of education and driven down proficiency.[11] Indeed, the progressives have made a complete shambles of the nation's finances. The government's fiscal operating debt now exceeds $20 trillion and unfunded liabilities exceed $200 trillion.[12] Meanwhile, the administrative state continues to issue rules and regulations by the tens of thousands, so many, in fact, that even the most engaged citizen cannot possibly know what they say or mean. Nonetheless, he is compelled to comply, under penalty of law.[13]

Yet, paradoxically, progressives insulate themselves from

effective reform or even criticism despite their endless writings about social experimentation and learned expertise. Their pursuit is undeniably ideological. Remember, progressives refute natural law—that is, the principle of eternal, transcendent moral law, truths, and knowledge—for they cannot control it. It is dismissed as either a passing historical footnote or an obstacle to societal progress, or is ridiculed as gibberish. They revile the Constitution's limits on unified, centralized power and its separation-of-powers formula.

Since the principles undergirding America's founding are beyond mortal law, they are beyond the reach of the progressives and the administrative state. Hence the war on the founding values, beliefs, and traditions was and is intended to, among other things, stop legitimate inquiry into and teaching of first principles or purposes. They are to be made intellectually and culturally off-limits. Consequently, what is left is only one acceptable and overarching agenda—the progressive agenda. The only relevant political and historical discussion is about progressive ideas and, more specifically, about their promotion—secularism, value relativism, social experimentation, unified political power—but never about slowing the pace or altering the main thrust and trajectory of progressivism. There can be no serious consideration of constitutional limits on the administrative state; no serious debate about governmental spending and debt; no serious argument about the "science" of climate change; no serious discussion of effective reforms for governmental entitlements and programs, such as Social Security, Medicare, or Obamacare; no serious thought of eliminating governmental departments and agencies. Ignorance is knowledge and centralized power is progress. In truth, however, it is progressivism that is "stuck in history" and intellectually exhausted.

The progressive's deliberate effort to denude the individual of his free will and uniqueness; to organize mankind by a growing and ubiquitous centralized authority and collective command into a conforming, uniform mass; and to reject right reason and sober circumspection about true reform of the progressive project despite its manifest failures and dangerous boundlessness, presents all the markings of a nihilistic, autocratic mentality—unsurprising considering its ideological roots. But the disastrous consequences for the individual cannot be overstated.

FIVE

# LIBERTY AND REPUBLICANISM

THIS LEADS US TO the next related and essential area of inquiry—what do we mean by human and individual freedom and how do we apply them in the context of what has been discussed thus far? While these issues are too large for an all-inclusive dissertation, they require concentrated treatment.

On April 4, 1819, in a letter replying to Isaac H. Tiffany, Thomas Jefferson succinctly described liberty: "Of liberty then I would say that, in the whole plenitude of its extent, it is unobstructed action according to our will: but rightful liberty is unobstructed action according to our will, within the limits drawn around us by the equal rights of others. I do not add 'within the limits of the law'; because law is often but the tyrant's will, and always so when it violates the right of an individual."[1] In this short statement, did Jefferson capture the essence of liberty?

Let us begin with John Stuart Mill, a distinguished British philosopher. I start here not because Mill had any influence on the Founders (an impossibility since he lived from 1806 to 1873) but because his utilitarian-libertarian writings are useful in understanding, developing, and discussing what is meant by liberty, a subject more multifaceted than one might at first imagine. Mill's book *On Liberty* (1859) has been prominent since its publication. He asked: "What . . . is the rightful limit to the sovereignty of the individual over himself? Where does the authority of society begin? How much of human life should be assigned to individuality, and how much to society?" Mill answered, in part, that "every one who receives the protection of society owes a return for the benefit, and the fact of living in society renders it indispensable that each should be found to observe a certain line of conduct towards the rest. This conduct consists, first, in not injuring the interest of one another; or rather certain interests, which, either by express legal provision or by tacit understanding, ought to be considered as rights; and secondly, in each person's bearing his share (to be fixed on some equitable principle) of the labors and sacrifices incurred for defending the society or its members from injury and molestation. . . . Nor is this all that society may do. . . . As soon as any part of a person's conduct affects prejudicially the interests of others, society has jurisdiction over it, and the question whether the general welfare will or will not be promoted by interfering with it, becomes open to discussion. But there is no room for entertaining any such question when a person's conduct affects the interests of no person besides himself, or needs not affect them unless they like. . . . In all such cases there should be perfect freedom, legal and social, to do the action and stand the consequences."[2]

Mill explained further that his utilitarianism is not a philosophy of isolated individualism or social disinterest: "It would be a great misunderstanding of this doctrine, to suppose that it is one of selfish indifference, which pretends that human beings have no business with each other's conduct in life, and that they should not concern themselves about the well-doing and well-being of one another, unless their own interest is involved. Instead of any diminution, there is need of a great increase in disinterested exertion to promote the good of others. But disinterested benevolence can find other instruments to persuade people of their good, than whips and scourges, either of the literal or metaphorical sort. . . ."[3] However, Mill added that "neither one person, nor any number of persons, is warranted in saying to another human creature of ripe years, that he shall not do with his life for his own benefit what he chooses to do. He is the person most interested in his own well-being; the interests which any other person, except in cases of strong personal attachment, can have in it, is trifling, compared with that which he himself has; the interest which society has in him individually (except as to his conduct to others) is fractional, and altogether indirect. . . .

Individuality has its proper field of action. In the conduct of human beings towards one another, it is necessary that general rules should for the most part be observed, in order that people may know what they have to expect; but in each person's own concerns, his individual spontaneity is entitled to free exercise. Considerations to aid his judgment, exhortations to strengthen his will, may be offered to him, even obtruded on him, by others; but he, himself, is the final judge. All errors which he is likely to commit against advice and warning, are far outweighed by the evil of allowing others to constrain him to what they deem his good."[4]

However, for Mill the ultimate end for the individual and society is happiness. In his 1863 essay, *Utilitarianism*, Chapter 2, he wrote: "The creed which accepts as the foundation of morals, Utility, or the Greatest Happiness Principle, holds that actions are right in proportion as they tend to promote happiness, wrong as they tend to produce the reverse of happiness. By happiness is intended pleasure, and the absence of pain; by unhappiness, pain, and the privation of pleasure. To give a clear view of the moral standard set up by the theory, much more requires to be said; in particular, what things it includes in the ideas of pain and pleasure; and to what extent this is left an open question. But these supplementary explanations do not affect the theory of life on which this theory of morality is grounded—namely, that pleasure, and freedom from pain, are the only things desirable as ends; and that all desirable things (which are as numerous in the utilitarian as in any other scheme) are desirable either for the pleasure inherent in themselves, or as means to the promotion of pleasure and the prevention of pain."[5]

Some criticized Mill's view as entirely hedonistic, to which Mill replied in *Utilitarianism*, Chapter 4:

> The utilitarian doctrine is, that happiness is desirable, and the only thing desirable, as an end; all other things being only desirable as means to that end. . . . But does the utilitarian doctrine deny that people desire virtue, or maintain that virtue is not a thing to be desired? The very reverse. It maintains not only that virtue is to be desired, but that it is to be desired disinterestedly, for itself. Whatever may be the opinion of utilitarian moralists as to the original conditions by which virtue is made virtue; however they may believe (as they do) that actions and dispositions are only virtuous because they promote another end than virtue; yet this being granted, and it having been decided, from considerations of this description, what is virtuous, they not only place virtue at the very head of the things which are good as means to the ultimate end, but they also recognize as a psychological fact the possibility of its being, to the individual, a good in itself, without looking to any end beyond it; and hold, that the mind is not in a right state, not in a state conformable to Utility, not in the state most conducive to the general happiness, unless it does love virtue in this

> manner—as a thing desirable in itself, even although, in the individual instance, it should not produce those other desirable consequences which it tends to produce, and on account of which it is held to be virtue. This opinion is not, in the smallest degree, a departure from the Happiness principle. The ingredients of happiness are very various, and each of them is desirable in itself, and not merely when considered as swelling an aggregate. The principle of utility does not mean that any given pleasure, as music, for instance, or any given exemption from pain, as for example health, is to be looked upon as means to a collective something termed happiness, and to be desired on that account. They are desired and desirable in and for themselves; besides being means, they are a part of the end. Virtue, according to the utilitarian doctrine, is not naturally and originally part of the end, but it is capable of becoming so; and in those who love it disinterestedly it has become so, and is desired and cherished, not as a means to happiness, but as a part of their happiness.[6]

The Declaration of Independence states that among the individual's "unalienable Rights" are "Life, Liberty and the pursuit of *Happiness*." It would seem that happiness, properly understood, coupled with virtue, was also a critical factor in the Founders' comprehension of liberty. For example, on December 10, 1819, in a fascinating letter to John Adams, Jefferson, while reflecting on the reasons for the demise of the

Roman Empire, described the basic elements of liberty and good government, with an emphasis on a *virtuous* people:

> I have been amusing myself latterly with reading the voluminous letters of Cicero. They certainly breathe the present effusions of an exalted patriot, while the parricide Caesar is left in odious contrast. When the enthusiasm however kindled by Cicero's pen & principles subsides into cool reflection, I ask myself what was that government which the virtues of Cicero were so zealous to restore, & the ambition of Caesar to subvert? And if Caesar had been as virtuous as he was daring and sagacious, what could he, even in the plentitude of his usurped power have done to lead his fellow citizens into good government? I do not say to restore it, because they never had it, from the rape of the Sabines to the ravages of the Caesars. If their people indeed had been, like ours, enlightened, peaceable, and really free, the answer would be obvious—"restore independence to all your foreign conquests, relieve Italy from the government of the rabble of Rome, consult it as a nation entitled to self-government, and do its will."
>
> But steeped in corruptive vice and venality as the whole nation was, (and nobody had done more than Caesar to corrupt it) what could even Cicero, Cato, Brutus have done, had it been referred to them to establish a good government for their country? They had no ideas of

government themselves but of their degenerate Senate, nor the people of liberty, but of the factious opposition of their tribunes. They had afterwards their Titusses, their Trajans, and Antoninuses, who had the will to make them happy, and the power to mould their government into a good and permanent form. But it would seem as if they could not see their way clearly to do it. No government can continue good but under the control of the people: and their people were so demoralized and depraved as to be incapable of exercising a wholesome control. Their reformation then was to be taken up ab incunabulis [from infancy]. Their minds were to be informed, by education, what is right & what wrong, to be encouraged in habits of virtue, & deterred from those of vice by the dread of punishments, proportioned indeed, but irremissibly; in all cases to follow truth as the only safe guide, & to eschew error . . . [which] bewilder us in one false consequence after another in endless succession.

These are the inculcations necessary to render the people a sure basis for the structure of order & good government, but this would have been an operation of a generation or two at least, within which period would have succeeded many Neros and Commoduses, who could have quashed the whole process. I confess then I can neither see what Cicero, Cato, & Brutus, united and uncontrolled, could have devised to lead their people into good government, nor how this enigma can be solved, nor how

> further shewn. Why it has been the fate of that delightful country never to have known to this day & through a course of five & twenty hundred years, the history of which we possess one single day of free & rational government. Your intimacy with their history, ancient, middle & modern, your familiarity with the improvements in the science of government at this time, will enable you, if any body, to go back with our principles & opinions to the times of Cicero, Cato, & Brutus, & tell us by what process these great & virtuous men could have led so unenlightened and vitiated a people into freedom & good government. . . .[7]

Hence, for Jefferson, and most of the Founders, virtue was an essential element of liberty; if the people lack virtue, no form of government can rescue them from tyranny. Again, it must be remembered that the Founders relied on the wisdom of such thinkers as Aristotle, Cicero, and Locke and were influenced by such contemporaries as Edmund Burke and Adam Smith, among others, all of whom spent considerable time contemplating virtue. And the Founders returned repeatedly to the importance of natural law, eternal truths, and the *transcendent moral order*, including virtue.

Indeed, French philosopher Charles de Montesquieu (1689–1755) and his book *The Spirit of the Laws* (1748) were widely embraced by the Founders, especially during the constitutional period. Montesquieu explained: "There are three kinds of government: REPUBLICAN, MONARCHICAL, AND DESPOTIC. To discover the nature of each, the idea of them held by the least educated of men is sufficient. I assume three definitions, or rather, three facts: one, republican government is that in which the people as a body, or only a part of the people, have sovereign power; monarchical government is that in which one alone governs, but by fixed and established law; whereas, in despotic government, one alone, without law and without rule, draws everything along by his will and caprices. . . . There need not be much integrity for monarchical or despotic government to maintain or sustain itself. The force of the law in the one and the prince's ever-raised arm in the other can rule or contain the whole. In a popular state there must be an additional spring, which is VIRTUE. What I say is confirmed by the entire body of history and is quite in conformity with the nature of things. For it is clear that less virtue is needed in a monarchy, where the one who sees to the execution of the laws judges himself above the laws, than in a popular government, where the one who sees to the execution of the laws feels that he is subject to them himself and that he will bear their weight. . . . But in a popular government when the laws have ceased to be executed, as this can come only from the corruption of the republic, the state is already lost."[8] In despotic government, "virtue is not at all necessary to it."[9]

Montesquieu saw despotism, including its frequent antecedent, anarchy, as a continuing threat. He explained: "When that virtue ceases, ambition enters those hearts that can admit it, and avarice enters them all. Desires change their objects: what which one used to love, one loves no longer. One was free under the laws, one wants to be free against them. Each citizen is like a slave who has escaped from his master's house. What was a *maxim* is now called *severity*; what was a *rule* is now called *constraint*; what was *vigilance* is now called *fear*. There, frugality, not the desire to possess, is avarice. Formerly the goods of individuals made up the public treasury; the public treasury has now become the patrimony of individuals. The republic is a cast-off husk, and its strength is no more than the power of a few citizens and the license to all."[10]

Starting in 1774, John Adams wrote a series of essays, the Novanglus essays, to his fellow Massachusetts Bay Colony citizens, which were published in the *Boston Gazette*. Among other things, Adams stressed the inextricable relationship between liberty and virtue. He wrote: "Liberty can no more exist without virtue and independence, than the body can live and move without a soul. When these are gone, and the popular branch of the constitution has become dependent on the minister, as it is in England, or cut off, as it is in America, all other forms of the constitution may remain; but if you look for liberty, you will grope in vain; and the freedom of the press, instead of promoting the cause of liberty, will but hasten its destruction, as the best cordials taken by patients in some distempers become the most rancid and corrosive poisons."[11]

In fact, the Virginia Declaration of Rights (June 12, 1776), drafted by George Mason, included this essential section:

"That no free government, or the blessings of liberty, can be preserved to any people but by a firm adherence to justice, moderation, temperance, frugality, and virtue and by frequent recurrence to fundamental principles."[12] The Pennsylvania Declaration of Rights (August 16, 1776), drafted primarily by Benjamin Franklin, similarly included a passage about virtue: "That a frequent recurrence to fundamental principles, and a firm adherence to justice, moderation, temperance, industry, and frugality are absolutely necessary to preserve the blessings of liberty, and keep a government free . . ."[13] And the Massachusetts Declaration of Rights (1780), whose authors included John and Samuel Adams, included a like provision: "A frequent recurrence to the fundamental principles of the Constitution, and a constant adherence to those of piety, justice, moderation, temperance, industry, and frugality, are absolutely necessary, to preserve the advantages of liberty, and to maintain a free government. . . ."[14]

As Russell Kirk (1918–1994), a major conservative thinker and historian, explained in his book *The Conservative Mind—from Burke to Eliot* (1953): "Liberty, in short, cannot be discussed in the abstract as if it were totally independent of public virtue and the framework of institutions. [John] Adams's knowledge that freedom is a delicate plant, that even watering it with the blood of martyrs is dubious nutriment, impels him to outline a practical system for liberty under law. Liberty must be under law; there is no satisfactory alternative; liberty without law endures so long as a lamb among wolves.

Even the compass of the civil laws does not sufficiently hedge liberty about: under cover of the best laws imaginable, freedom may still be infringed if virtue is lacking. What sort of government, then, will stimulate this indispensable private and public virtue comprehended in the golden rule?"[15] A constitutional republic, of course.

Consequently, there must be a legal order, informed by a moral order, if the individual is to flourish. The wrong human-made law—which is contrary to or rejects natural rights—is oppressive. The right kind of law, adopted for the right reasons and in the right manner through republican institutions, can certainly help secure and even nurture individual and societal liberty, at least for a time.

Mill witnessed the growing influence and tyrannical threat of the so-called reformers and what would later include the progressives and he addressed them: "[S]ome of those modern reformers who have placed themselves in strongest opposition to the religions of the past, have been no way behind either churches or sects in their assertion of the right of spiritual domination. . . . [Their] aims at establishing . . . a despotism of society over the individual, surpass[es] anything contemplated in the political ideal of the most rigid disciplinarian among the ancient philosophers."[16] In fact, as Mill was writing his books and essays, the ideologies of Rousseau, Hegel, and Marx, among others, were taking tangible, political form at the urging of intellectuals throughout the world, including in the West. "Apart from the peculiar tenets of individual thinkers, there is also in the world at large an increasing inclination to stretch unduly the power of society over the individual, both by the force of opinion and even by that of legislation: and as the tendency of all the changes taking place in the world is to strengthen society, and diminish the power of the individual, this encroachment is not one of the evils which tend spontaneously to disappear, but, on the contrary, to grow more and more formidable. This disposition of mankind, whether as rulers or as fellow-citizens, to impose their own opinions and inclinations as a rule of conduct on others, is so energetically supported by some of the best and by some of the worst feelings incident to human nature, that it is hardly ever kept under restraint by anything but want of power; and as the power is not declining, but growing, unless a strong barrier of moral conviction can be raised against the mischief, we must expect, in the present circumstances of the world, to see it increase."[17]

In more recent times, the Russian-British political theorist and philosopher Isaiah Berlin (1909–1997) examined liberty by dividing it into two general but distinct categories—positive liberty and negative liberty. As will become clear, these are easily confused terms, suggesting that "positive" liberty is something that is good and "negative" liberty is something that is bad; or perhaps that "positive" liberty establishes liberty and "negative" liberty denies it. That is not the case. Indeed, I would contend that the contrary is mostly true.

In various lectures and writings beginning in the 1950s, Berlin went further in developing these analytical devices.

He explained that positive liberty "is involved in the answer to the question 'What, or who, is the source of control or interference that can determine someone to do, or be, this rather than that?' The two questions are clearly different, even though the answers to them may overlap."[18] Conversely, "liberty in the negative sense involves an answer to the question 'What is the area within which the subject—a person or group of persons—is or should be left to do or be what he is able to do or be, without interference by other persons.'"[19] The *Stanford Encyclopedia of Philosophy* describes the concepts straightforwardly: "Negative liberty is the absence of obstacles, barriers or constraints. One has negative liberty to the extent that actions are available to one in this negative sense. Positive liberty is the possibility of acting—or the fact of acting—in such a way as to take control of one's life and realize one's fundamental purposes. While negative liberty is usually attributed to individual agents, positive liberty is sometimes attributed to collectivities, or to individuals considered primarily as members of given collectivities."[20] "The reason for using these labels is that in the first case liberty seems to be a mere *absence* of something (i.e., of obstacles, barriers, constraints or interference from others), whereas in the second case it seems to require the *presence* of something (i.e., of control, self-mastery, self-determination or self-realization)."[21]

Throughout the discussion of progressivism—from Rousseau, Hegel, and Marx to Croly, Roosevelt, Wilson, Dewey, and Weyl—the core themes have evolved around defining individual worth, salvation, and liberation through the lenses of the collective, scientifically managed by and through a centralized, unified governmental construct (often referred to or compared to a living organism or body) said to represent the general will, general welfare, national interests, and working masses (proletariat). "This organism will only act rationally, will only be in control of itself, when its various parts are brought into line with some rational plan devised by its wise governors (who, to extend the metaphor, might be thought of as the organism's brain). In this case, even the majority might be oppressed in the name of liberty."[22] However, what is missing all through is an appreciation for and the best interests of the sanctity and sovereignty of the unique, flesh-and-blood, individual human being.

In his 1958 Inaugural Lecture on the two concepts of liberty, and its follow-up essays, Berlin explained that studies about politics and philosophy in academia "spring from, and thrive on, discord. Someone may question this on the ground that even in a society of saintly anarchists, where no conflicts about ultimate purposes can take place, political problems, for example constitutional or legislative issues, might still arise. But this objection rests on a mistake. Where ends are agreed, the only questions left are those of means, and these are not political but technical, that is to say, capable of being settled by experts or machines, like arguments between engineers or doctors. That is why those who put their faith in some immense, world-transforming phenomenon, like the final triumph of reason or the proletarian revolution, must believe that all political and moral problems can thereby be turned into technological ones. That is the meaning of Engels' famous phrase (paraphrasing Saint-Simon) about 'replacing the government of persons by the administration of things,' and the Marxist prophecies about the withering away of the State and the beginning of the true history of humanity. This outlook is called Utopian by those for whom speculation about this condition of perfect social harmony is the play of idle fancy. Nevertheless, a visitor from Mars to any British—or American—university today might perhaps be forgiven if he sustained the impression that its members lived in something very like this innocent and idyllic state, for all the serious attention that is paid to fundamental problems of politics by professional philosophers."[23]

In this, Berlin said that the people ignore the academics and intellectuals at their own peril since it is they who devise and develop the philosophical and political notions upon which politics is practiced. And politics, in turn, is the means by which institutions govern and affect society and the individual. Consequently, Berlin exhorted that not enough attention is paid to this debate and the debaters despite the fact that the outcome will determine the future of humanity. "Yet this is both surprising and dangerous. Surprising because there has, perhaps, been no time in modern history when so large a number of human beings, in both the East and the

West, have had their notions, and indeed their lives, so deeply altered, and in some cases violently upset, by fanatically held social and political doctrines. Dangerous, because when ideas are neglected by those who ought to attend to them—that is to say, those who have been trained to think critically about ideas—they sometimes acquire an unchecked momentum and an irresistible power over multitudes of men that may grow too violent to be affected by rational criticism. Over a hundred years ago, the German poet Heine warned the French not to underestimate the power of ideas: philosophical concepts nurtured in the stillness of a professor's study could destroy a civilization."[24]

In further describing negative liberty, Berlin argued: "I am normally said to be free to the degree to which no man or body of men interferes with my activity. Political liberty in this sense is simply the area within which a man can act unobstructed by others. If I am prevented by others from doing what I could otherwise do, I am to that degree unfree; and if this area is contracted by other men beyond a certain minimum, I can be described as being coerced, or, it may be, enslaved. Coercion is not, however, a term that covers every form of inability. If I say that I am unable to jump more than ten feet in the air, or cannot read because I am blind, or cannot understand the darker pages of Hegel, it would be eccentric to say that I am to that degree enslaved or coerced. Coercion implies the deliberate interference of other human beings within the area in which I could otherwise act. You lack political liberty or freedom only if you are prevented from attaining a goal by human beings. Mere incapacity to attain a goal is not lack of political freedom."[25]

Berlin then analyzed the state of mind motivating modern progressives: "What troubles the consciences of Western liberals is . . . the belief, not that the freedom that men seek differs according to their social or economic conditions, but that the minority who possess it have gained it by exploiting, or, at least, averting their gaze from, the vast majority who do not. They believe, with good reason, that if individual liberty is an ultimate end for human beings, none should be deprived of it by others; least of all that some should enjoy it at the expense of others. Equality of liberty; not to treat others as I should not wish them to treat me; repayment of my debt to those who alone have made possible my liberty or prosperity or enlightenment; justice, in its simplest and most universal sense—these are the foundations of liberal morality. . . . But nothing is gained by a confusion of terms. To avoid glaring inequality or widespread misery I am ready to sacrifice some, or all, of my freedom: I may do so willingly and freely; but it is freedom that I am giving up for the sake of justice or equality or the love of my fellow men. I should be guilt-stricken, and rightly so, if I were not, in some circumstances, ready to make this sacrifice. But a sacrifice is not an increase in what is being sacrificed, namely freedom, however great the moral need or the compensation for it. . . . Yet it remains true that the freedom of some must at times be curtailed to secure the freedom of others. Upon what principle should this be done? If freedom is a sacred, untouchable value, there can be no such principle. One or other of these conflicting rules or principles must, at any rate in practice, yield: not always for reasons which can be clearly stated, let alone generalized into rules or universal maxims. Still, a practical compromise has to be found."[26]

Turning to the positive liberty concept, Berlin asserted: "Self-government may, on the whole, provide a better guarantee of the preservation of civil liberties than other regimes, and has been defended as such by libertarians. But there is no necessary connection between individual liberty and democratic rule. The answer to the question 'Who governs me?' is logically distinct from the question 'How far does government interfere with me?' It is in this difference that the great contrast between the two concepts of negative and positive liberty, in the end, consists. For the 'positive' sense of liberty comes to light if we try to answer the question, not 'What am I free to do or be?' but 'By whom am I ruled?' or 'Who is to say what I am, and what I am not, to be or do?' The connection between democracy and individual liberty is a good deal more tenuous than it seemed to many advocates of both. The desire to be governed by myself, or at any rate to participate in the process by which my life is to be controlled, may be as deep a wish as that for a free area for action, and perhaps historically older. But it is not a desire for the same thing. So different is it, indeed, as to have led in the end to the great clash of ideologies that dominates our world. For it is this, the 'positive' conception of liberty, not freedom *from*, but freedom *to*—to lead one prescribed form of life—which the adherents of the 'negative' notion represent as being, at times, no better than a specious disguise for brutal tyranny."[27]

Moreover, and notably, Berlin describes the mind-set of modern progressives and their philosophical patrons, declaring that in exercising the positive freedom idea *to* be all you want to be, the danger is that "the real self may be conceived as something wider than the individual (as the term is normally understood), as a social 'whole' of which the individual is an element or aspect: a tribe, a race, a Church, a State, the great society of the living and the dead and the yet unborn. This entity is then identified as being the 'true' self which, by imposing its collective, or 'organic,' single will upon its recalcitrant 'members,' achieves its own, and therefore their, 'higher' freedom. The perils of using organic metaphors [general will of the people, general welfare of the people, etc.] to justify the coercion of some men by others in order to raise them to a 'higher' level of freedom have often been pointed out. But what gives such plausibility as it has to this kind of language is that we recognize that it is possible, and at times justifiable, to coerce men in the name of some goal (let us say, justice or public health) which they would, if they were more enlightened, themselves pursue, but do not, because they are blind or ignorant or corrupt. This renders it easy for me to conceive of myself as coercing others for their own sake, in their, not my interest. [. . .] [T]hey would not resist me if they were rational and as wise as I, and understood their interests as I do."[28]

As Berlin explained further: "I may go on to claim a good deal more than this. I may declare that they are actually aiming at what in their benighted state they consciously resist, because there exists within them an occult entity—their latent rational will, or their 'true' purpose—and that this entity, although it is belied by all that they overtly feel and do and say, is their 'real' self, of which the poor empirical self in space and time may know nothing or little; and that this inner spirit is the only self that deserves to have its wishes taken into account. Once I take this view, I am in a position to ignore the actual wishes of men or societies, to bully, oppress, torture them in the name, and on behalf, of their 'real' selves, in the secure knowledge that whatever is the true goal of man (happiness, performance of duty, wisdom, a just society, self-fulfillment) must be identical with his freedom—the free choice of his 'true,' albeit often submerged and inarticulate, self."[29]

Berlin was also well aware of the calculating psychology and behavior of the autocratic masterminds, among whom I include the progressives. "[T]he 'positive' conception of freedom as self-mastery, with its suggestion of a man divided against himself, has in fact, and as a matter of history, of doctrine and of practice, lent itself more easily to this splitting of personality into two: the transcendent, dominant controller,

and the empirical bundle of desires and passions to be disciplined and brought to heel. It is this historical fact that has been influential. This demonstrates (if demonstration of so obvious a truth is needed) that conceptions of freedom directly derive from views of what constitutes a self, a person, a man. Enough manipulation of the definition of man, and freedom can be made to mean whatever the manipulator wishes. Recent history has made it only too clear that the issue is not merely academic."[30]

Irish philosopher and Princeton University professor Philip Pettit has also spent considerable time examining and writing about the issue of freedom. In his book *Republicanism: A Theory of Freedom and Government* (1997), Pettit, among other things, examined certain ancient thinkers as well as American Revolutionary period writers. He asserts: "The important point to notice . . . is that the writers . . . take liberty to be defined by a status in which the evils associated with interference are avoided [negative liberty] rather than by access to the instruments of democratic control [positive liberty], participatory or representative. Democratic control is certainly important in the tradition, but its importance comes, not from any definitional connection with liberty, but from the fact that it is a means of furthering liberty."[31]

Of course, sometime after the American Revolution, when the framers undertook the task of drafting the Constitution, the preamble, although merely introductory and adopted near the end of the Constitutional Convention, declared formally

and publicly the official purpose of their task: "We the People of the United States, in Order to form a more perfect Union, establish Justice, insure domestic Tranquility, provide for the common defence, promote the general Welfare, and secure the Blessings of Liberty to ourselves and our Posterity, do ordain and establish this Constitution for the United States of America."[32] As Pettit contends, the framers did so to secure and promote individual liberty and the civil society.

Pettit also explains that some of the founding-era writers supported a populist approach to government, favoring majoritarianism (meaning a democratic form of government) to republicanism, and that such a governing construct actually threatens the safeguards against arbitrary interference with individual liberty. "While it is true that the republican thinkers [meaning those who believe in a republican form of government] in general regarded democratic participation or representation as a safeguard of liberty, not as its defining core, the growing emphasis on democracy did lead some individuals away from traditional alignments and towards the full populist position of holding that liberty consists in nothing more than democratic self-rule. . . . Rousseau is probably responsible for having given currency to such a populist view. The populist twist was a new development, and attained its full form only when the ideal of democratic self-rule came to be held up as the main alternative, or at least the main alternative among notions of liberty, to the negative ideal of non-interference. To think of the republican tradition as populist, as of course

many have done, would be to sustain the very dichotomy that has rendered the republican ideal invisible."[33]

This new "populism" certainly was not the dominant view during America's founding. The entire debate surrounding the drafting, adoption, and ratification of the Constitution, and the debates between the Federalists and Anti-Federalists, make this abundantly clear. As discussed earlier and at length, however, the progressives did and do use populist language and appeals to nationalism to make alluring the promotion of an ever larger and more centralized governmental presence and administrative structure. Their approach could be characterized as democratizing tyranny. Progressives condemn America's founding principles, including the Declaration of Independence and its emphasis on individual unalienable rights, as well as the Constitution, especially the separation-of-powers doctrine and federalism, precisely because of their republican features and obstacles to concentrated governmental power.

Pettit takes a somewhat different view than Berlin in that he contends the republican emphasis on avoiding interference did not come as a belief in freedom as noninterference but as a belief in freedom as *nondomination*. "There are two grounds for thinking that the conception of liberty as nondomination is the view of liberty that we find in the republican tradition. This first is that in the republican tradition, by contrast with the modernist [progressive] approach, liberty is always cast in terms of opposition between . . . citizen and slave. The condition of liberty is explicated as the status of someone who, unlike the slave, is not subject to the arbitrary power of another; that is, someone who is not dominated by anyone else. Thus, the condition of liberty is explicated in such a way that there may be a loss of liberty without any actual interference: there may be enslavement and domination without interference, as in the scenario of the non-interfering master. . . . The second ground is that liberty is explicated within the republican tradition in such a way that not only can liberty be lost without actual interference; equally, interference may occur, under the scenario of the non-mastering interferer, without people being rendered thereby unfree. The non-mastering interferer envisaged by republicans . . . was the law and government that obtains in a well-ordered republic."[34]

Pettit contends that "the interference-without-domination motif comes out in the republican emphasis on the fact that while the properly constituted law—the law that answers systematically to people's general interests and ideas—represents a form of interference, it does not compromise people's liberty; it constitutes a non-mastering interferer."[35] "According to the earliest republican doctrine, the laws of a suitable state, in particularly the laws of a republic, create the freedom enjoyed by citizens; they do not offend against that freedom, even in a measure for which they later compensate. . . . As the laws create the authority that rulers enjoy, so the laws create the freedom that citizens share. The laws only do this, of course, so long as they respect people's common interests and ideas and conform to the image of an ideal law; so long as they are not the instruments of any individual's, or any group's, arbitrary will. When the laws become the instruments of will, according to the tradition, then we have a regime—say, the despotic regime of the absolute king—in which the citizens become slaves and are entirely deprived of their freedom. . . ."[36]

Pettit argues the republican view holds that "[g]ood laws may relieve people from domination—may protect them against the resources or *dominium* of those who would otherwise have arbitrary power over them—without themselves introducing any new dominating force; without introducing the domination that can go with governmental *imperium*. The political authorities recognized by the laws represent potential dominators, but the recurrent republican idea is that these will themselves be suitably constrained—they will have no arbitrary power over others—under a proper constitution; say, where suitable mechanisms and representation, rotation of office, separation of powers, and like are in place. While the law necessarily involves interference—while law is essentially coercive—the interference in question is not going to be arbitrary; the legal authorities will be entitled and enabled to interfere only when pursuing the common interests of citizens and only when pursuing these in a manner that conforms to the opinions received among the citizenry."[37]

However, Berlin's negative liberty of noninterventionism and Pettit's modification of interventionism to nondomination are not necessarily in conflict. Instead, I believe that both, taken together with virtue, represent the intent and approach of the American Founders. There are essential areas of individual liberty that should remain unmolested by man-made entities like government, and there are other areas where there may be intervention, including of the nondominant sort. The drawing of lines is relevant only within the framework of natural law considerations, civil society compacts, and a republican governing system. (Tyrannical regimes are built on notions of positive liberty, where such line drawing is less relevant because individualism is less relevant.)

For example, negative liberty, both noninterventionist and nondominant, are present in the Constitution's Bill of Rights. It is a set of negative liberty directives to the federal government, where the federal government is prevented from taking certain actions altogether, or where actions are to be limited in scope.

> Amendment I
> Congress shall make no law respecting an establishment of religion, or prohibiting the free exercise thereof; or abridging the freedom of speech, or of the press; or the right of the people peaceably to assemble, and to petition the government for a redress of grievances.
>
> Amendment II
> A well regulated militia, being necessary to the security of a free state, the right of the people to keep and bear arms, shall not be infringed.

Amendment III

No soldier shall, in time of peace be quartered in any house, without the consent of the owner, nor in time of war, but in a manner to be prescribed by law.

Amendment IV

The right of the people to be secure in their persons, houses, papers, and effects, against unreasonable searches and seizures, shall not be violated, and no warrants shall issue, but upon probable cause, supported by oath or affirmation, and particularly describing the place to be searched, and the persons or things to be seized.

Amendment V

No person shall be held to answer for a capital, or otherwise infamous crime, unless on a presentment or indictment of a grand jury, except in cases arising in the land or naval forces, or in the militia, when in actual service in time of war or public danger; nor shall any person be subject for the same offense to be twice put in jeopardy of life or limb; nor shall be compelled in any criminal case to be a witness against himself, nor be deprived of life, liberty, or property, without due process of law; nor shall private property be taken for public use, without just compensation.

Amendment VI

In all criminal prosecutions, the accused shall enjoy the right to a speedy and public trial, by an impartial jury of the state and district wherein the crime shall have been committed, which district shall have been previously ascertained by law, and to be informed of the nature and cause of the accusation; to be confronted with the witnesses against him; to have compulsory process for obtaining witnesses in his favor, and to have the assistance of counsel for his defense.

Amendment VII

In suits at common law, where the value in controversy shall exceed twenty dollars, the right of trial by jury shall be preserved, and no fact tried by a jury, shall be otherwise reexamined in any court of the United States, than according to the rules of the common law.

Amendment VIII

Excessive bail shall not be required, nor excessive fines imposed, nor cruel and unusual punishments inflicted.

Amendment IX

The enumeration in the Constitution, of certain rights, shall not be construed to deny or disparage others retained by the people.

> Amendment X
>
> The powers not delegated to the United States by the Constitution, nor prohibited by it to the states, are reserved to the states respectively, or to the people.[38]

Of course, for the progressive, none of this is of consequence. The progressive believes in a spiritual and actual slavery to mankind's perfectibility by mankind itself. The American heritage is considered a heritage of folklore and irrelevance, if not regressive and obstructive. Therefore, for the progressive, reason alone, the here and now, science applied to human behavior and governance, the individual as community, and the existing social needs require a "higher nature." And that higher nature is of modern man's making, unencumbered by external truth, the guidance and constraints of a moral order, or ancient traditions. Again, as Berlin said, the question then is not about the individual's liberty but is "What, or who, is the source of control or interference that can determine someone to do, or be, this rather than that?"[39] For the progressive, the answer is the centralized administrative state, where the individual is coerced in infinite ways, as willed by the machinery of the state. As such, reason transforms into will, which in turn transforms into an ideological pursuit of control and power. Actual science, reason, and knowledge are abandoned. Yet this is said to be liberating of both the individual and society. Mankind is said to be free and autonomous when, in fact, the opposite is true. Berlin wrote: "But to manipulate men, to propel them towards goals which you—the social reformer—see, but they may not, is to deny their human essence, to treat them as objects without wills of their own, and therefore to degrade them. That is why to lie to men, or to deceive them, that is, to use them as means for my, not their own, independently conceived ends, even if it is for their own benefit, is, in effect, to treat them as subhuman, to behave as if their ends are less ultimate and sacred than my own. . . ."[40] Berlin explained: "If I find that I am able to do little or nothing of what I wish, I need only contract or extinguish my wishes, and I am made free. If the tyrant (or 'hidden persuader') manages to condition his subjects (or customers) into losing their original wishes and embracing ('internalizing') the form of life he has invented for them, he will, on this definition, have succeeded in liberating them. He will, no doubt, have made them *feel* free. . . . But what he has created is the very antithesis of political freedom."[41]

Having rejected natural law and constitutional republicanism, the progressive embraces another theory of law, although foreign to the American heritage—*positive law*. Again, the word *positive* should not be confused with "the good" or promoting and securing liberty. Positive law is coercive law, law promulgated by the state to further the will and the purposes of the state. There is no moral basis or virtue tied to the law. The merits of the law are not material. In fact, such considerations are irrelevant. The government issues laws, rules, orders, or regulations and they are to be obeyed under threat of punishment. There is, then, a tension when the will of the state conflicts with the will of the people. However, for the progressive, external political influences, like elections, are nonlegal in nature. The state will determine if, and the extent to which, such nonlegal influences are worthy of consideration when developing, issuing, and enforcing the law. That said, as the very character of the government becomes less republican and more regime oriented, elections and other forms of popular and representative participation are less consequential. The ideologically driven "scientific"-based judgment of the administrative state, which has assumed much of the lawmaking authority of a legislature, ultimately prevails as it is unhinged from moral roots and grows increasingly immune from nonlegal influences.

At its core, positive law is an outgrowth of the doctrine of *positivism*, which in turn is a rejection of natural law. All knowledge is allegedly based on the relationships between and among phenomena resulting from empiricism and scientism. Auguste Comte (1798–1857), a French philosopher who is said by some to have originated the modern concept of positivism and the practice of sociology, wrote in his book *A General View of Positivism* (1848) that "[p]ositivism consists essentially of a Philosophy and a Polity [that is, an ideology and societal organization]. These can never be dissevered; the former being the basis, and the latter the end of one comprehensive system, in which our intellectual faculties and our social sympathies are brought into close correlation with each other. For, in the first place, the science of Society, besides being more important than any other, supplies the only logical and scientific link by which all our varied observations of phenomena can be brought into one consistent whole. . . ."[42]

Comte and John Stuart Mill were contemporaries. Mill wrote a book, *Auguste Comte and Positivism* (1865), in which Mill critiqued positivism and, specifically, condemned Comte's thinking. Mill explained that positivism is the general belief that "[w]e have no knowledge of anything but Phenomena [perception or happenings]; and our knowledge of phenomena is relative, not absolute. We know not the essence, nor the real mode of production, of any fact, but only its relations to other facts in the way of succession or of similitude. These relations are constant; that is, always the same in the same circumstances. The constant resemblances which link phenomena together, and the constant sequences which unite them as antecedent and consequent, are termed their laws. The laws of phenomena are all we know respecting them. Their essential nature, and their ultimate causes, either efficient or final, are unknown and inscrutable to us. . . . Now, all foresight of phenomena, and power over them, depend on knowledge of their sequences, and not upon any notion we may have formed respecting their origin or inmost nature. . . . All foresight, therefore, and all intelligent action, have only been possible in proportion as men have successfully attempted to ascertain the successions of phenomena. Neither foreknowledge, nor the knowledge which is practical power, can be acquired by any other means."[43]

For Comte and his followers of scientism, this meant and means much more than destroying theology; it discards all notions of eternal truths and transcendent principles. "The theological synthesis depended exclusively upon our affective nature; and to this is owing its original supremacy and its ultimate decline. For a long time its influence over all our highest speculations was paramount. . . . In my work on Positive Philosophy I have clearly proved that it constitutes only a transitory phase of mind, and is totally inadequate for any constructive purpose. For a time it was supreme; but its utility lay simply in its revolutionary tendencies. It aided the preliminary development of Humanity by its gradual inroads upon Theology, which, though in ancient times entrusted with the sole direction of society, had long since become in every respect utterly retrograde."[44]

Comte's positivism and "stages of development" theory and the Hegel-Marx historicism are kindred and lay the foundation for modern progressivism. They all presume to know and establish the final stage of human development (even if the final stage is in a state of constant remaking), denounce organized religion and timeless truths, and worship the narcissism of their own moral nihilism. Indeed, Comte committed an entire chapter to the proposition of positivism-scientism-secularism as "the religion of humanity." "Love, then, is our principle; Order our basis; and Progress our end. Such . . . is the essential character of the system of life which Positivism offers for the definite acceptance of society; a system which regulates the whole course of our private and public existence, by bringing Feeling, Reason, and Activity into permanent harmony. In this final synthesis, all essential conditions are far more perfectly fulfilled than in any other. Each special element of our nature is more fully developed, and at the same time the general working of the whole is coherent. Greater distinctiveness is given to the truth that the affective element predominates in our nature. Life in all its actions and thoughts is brought under the control and inspiring charm of Social Sympathy." Comte added: "Public and private life are now brought into close relation by the identity of their principal aim, which, being kept constantly in sight, ennobles every action of both."[45] As with Rousseau, for Comte the individual realizes his fulfillment only as part of the whole community—that is, as a functionary of the state.

Positive liberty, positive law, and positivism are an ideological brew of tyranny. The pursuit of the "final stage" of human development grows miserable and ultimately elusive. Consequently, as mentioned earlier, positivism preaches ignorance of the ultimate meaning of law and absolute compliance with the state's ends. It requires a governing process of rules, demands, and adherence. The individual is subservient and submissive. He has no meaningful recourse. For example, as explored in my books *Liberty and Tyranny* and *Plunder and Deceit*, in present day, "man-made climate change" is declared by the state to be a scientific fact, around which the economy is to be reorganized and about which society is to be indoctrinated. Those who question not just the "science" but the motivations behind the movement are publicly denounced and ridiculed as "deniers." All contrary scientific evidence and knowledge are dismissed outright. The state has spoken and all shall obey.

As a result of these influences, over the last century there has been a thoroughgoing change in American jurisprudence and the legal system—and, therefore, in liberty itself. Specifically, the progressive's ideology is not only omnipresent in lawmaking through the administrative state, but is the overwhelmingly dominant approach to adjudication. In other words, more and more the law is as the progressive ideology dictates—a force for societal transformation and social reorganization. The banishment of the Constitution and republicanism, like the disembowelment of the Declaration of Independence and individualism, has been scrupulous. There is now a vast gulf between the government the progressives have constructed and the framers' Constitution.

In his book *The Ideological Origins of the American Revolution* (1967), the American historian and professor Bernard Bailyn writes, "The theory of politics that emerges from the political literature of the pre-Revolutionary years rests on the belief that what lay behind every political scene, the ultimate explanation of every political controversy, was the disposition of power. The acuteness of the colonists' sense of this problem is, for the [modern] reader, one of the most striking things to be found in the eighteenth-century literature: it serves to link the Revolutionary generation to our own in the most intimate way. The colonists had no doubt about what power was and about its central, dynamic role in any political system. . . . What gave transcendent importance to the aggressiveness of power was the fact that its natural prey, its necessary victim, was liberty, or law, or right. The public world these writers saw was divided into distinct, contrasting, and innately antagonistic spheres: the sphere of power and the sphere of liberty and right. The one was brutal, ceaselessly active, and heedless; the other was delicate, passive, and sensitive. . . . Not that power was in itself—in some metaphysical sense—evil. It was natural in its origins, and necessary. It had legitimate foundations 'in compact and mutual consent'—in those covenants among men by which, as a result of restrictions voluntarily accepted by all for the good of all, society emerges from a state of nature and creates government to serve as trustee and custodian of the mass of surrendered individual powers."[46]

The Founders were no less concerned that the federal government they were establishing would avoid the institutionalized abuses of power of other postrevolutionary societies. In this effort they strived mightily, and in this regard they looked to, among others, the wisdom of French philosopher Montesquieu and his seminal work, *The Spirit of the Laws*. Montesquieu discussed the nature of man, societies, and government. He explained that "[i]n despotic states, the nature of the government requires extreme obedience, and the prince's

will, once known, should produce its effect as infallibly as does one ball thrown against another. No tempering, modification, accommodation, terms, alternatives, negotiations, remonstrances, nothing as good or better can be proposed. Man is a creature that obeys a creature that wants. He can no more express his fears about a future event than he can blame his lack of success on the caprice of fortune. There, men's portion, like beasts', is instinct, obedience, and chastisement. It is useless to counter with natural feelings, respect for father, tenderness of one's children or women, laws of honor, of the state of one's health; one has received the order and that is enough."[47] In this, has Montesquieu not described the basic character of the progressives and their ideological forefathers?

Montesquieu also argued that for much of humankind, despotic governments have prevailed. "Despite men's love of liberty, despite their hatred of violence, most peoples are subjected to this type of government. This is easy to understand. In order to form a moderate government, one must combine powers, regulate them, temper them, make them act; one must give one power a ballast, so to speak, to put it in a position to resist another; this is a masterpiece of legislation that chance rarely produces and prudence is rarely allowed to produce. By contrast, despotic government leaps to view, so to speak; it is uniform throughout; as only passions are needed to establish it, everyone is good enough for that."[48] Again, is Montesquieu not forecasting the progressives' war on the separation-of-powers doctrine?

Even democracies are susceptible to tyrannies of a certain kind. Montesquieu wrote: "The principle of democracy is corrupted not only when the spirit of equality is lost but also when the spirit of extreme equality is taken up and each one wants to be the equal of those chosen to command. So the people, finding intolerable even the power they entrust to others, want to do everything themselves: to deliberate for the senate, to execute for the magistrates, and to cast aside all judges." Therefore, "democracy has to avoid two excesses: the spirit of inequality, which leads it to aristocracy or to the government of one alone, and the spirit of extreme equality, which leads it to the despotism of one alone, as the despotism of one alone ends by conquest."[49]

The progressive has succeeded in both regards by claiming to emancipate the individual through the democratization of autocracy—that is, justifying the concentration of governing power and the coercive envelopment of the individual with images of extreme egalitarianism and utopian promises.

For Montesquieu, like the framers, a republican government that was established by a fixed constitution, with the three powers of government—legislative, executive, and adjudicative—separated one from the other, provided the conditions for either creating or maintaining a free and civil society. He profoundly asserted that "[p]olitical liberty in a citizen is that tranquility of spirit which comes from the opinion each one has of his security, and in order for him to have this liberty the government must be such that one citizen cannot

fear another citizen." He went on to famously state the structure of such a government. "When legislative power is united with executive power in a single person or in a simple body of magistracy, there is no liberty, because one can fear that the same monarch or senate that makes tyrannical laws will execute them tyrannically. Nor is there liberty if the power of judging is not separate from the legislative power and from the executive power. If it were joined to the legislative power, the power over the life and liberty of the citizens would be arbitrary, for the judge would be the legislator. If it were joined to the executive power, the judge could have the force of an oppressor. All would be lost if the same man or the same body of principal men, either of nobles, or of the people, exercised these three powers: that of making the laws, that of executing public resolutions, and that of judging the crimes or the disputes of individuals."[50]

Obviously, this construct of separating the powers of government for the purpose of preventing centralized despotism was absolutely fundamental to the framers. It is one of two major innovations incorporated into America's republican system of constitutional government, the other being federalism. Indeed, the first three articles of the Constitution make this clear. Article I, Section 1: "All legislative Powers herein granted shall be vested in a Congress of the United States, which shall consist of a Senate and House of Representatives"; Article II, Section 1: "The executive Power shall be vested in a President of the United States of America"; Article III,

Section 1: "The judicial Power of the United States shall be vested in one supreme Court, and in such inferior Courts as the Congress may from time to time ordain and establish."[51]

During the subsequent state ratification debates, James Madison, Alexander Hamilton, and John Jay, all of whom had been delegates to the Constitutional Convention, famously penned and had published a series of brilliant essays later known as the *Federalist Papers*, in which they explained and defended the various provisions of the proposed Constitution, including the separation-of-powers structure.

In *Federalist* 47 (February 1, 1788), Madison underscored Montesquieu's view:

> The accumulation of all powers, legislative, executive, and judiciary, in the same hands, whether of one, a few, or many, and whether hereditary, self-appointed, or elective, may justly be pronounced the very definition of tyranny. Were the federal Constitution, therefore, really chargeable with the accumulation of power, or with a mixture of powers, having a dangerous tendency to such an accumulation, no further arguments would be necessary to inspire a universal reprobation of the system. I persuade myself, however, that it will be made apparent to every one, that the charge cannot be supported, and that the maxim on which it relies has been totally misconceived and misapplied. In order to form correct ideas on this important subject, it will be proper to investigate the sense

> in which the preservation of liberty requires that the three great departments of power should be separate and distinct. The oracle who is always consulted and cited on this subject is the celebrated Montesquieu.[52]

In addition, in *Federalist* 51 (February 6, 1788), Madison wrote:

> [T]he great security against a gradual concentration of the several powers in the same department, consists in giving to those who administer each department, the necessary constitutional means, and personal motives, to resist encroachments of the others. The provision for defense must in this, as in all other cases, be made commensurate to the danger of attack. Ambition must be made to counteract ambition. The interest of the man must be connected with the constitutional rights of the place. It may be a reflection on human nature, that such devices should be necessary to control the abuses of government. But what is government itself but the greatest of all reflections on human nature? If men were angels, no government would be necessary. If angels were to govern men, neither external nor internal controls on government would be necessary. In framing a government which is to be administered by men over men, the great difficulty lies in this: You must first enable the government to control the governed; and in the next place, oblige it to control it-

> self. A dependence on the people is no doubt the primary control on the government; but experience has taught mankind the necessity of auxiliary precautions.
>
> This policy of supplying by opposite and rival interests, the defect of better motives, might be traced through the whole system of human affairs, private as well as public. We see it particularly displayed in all the subordinate distributions of power; where the constant aim is to divide and arrange the several offices in such a manner as that each may be a check on the other; that the private interest of every individual, may be a sentinel over the public rights. These inventions of prudence cannot be less requisite in the distribution of the supreme powers of the state.[53]

The second unique but crucial character of the Constitution was federalism. As a practical matter, since the states created the federal government in the first place, much care was given by the delegates to the Constitution Convention and the delegates to the state ratification conventions to protecting areas of state sovereignty from federal and national encroachment. Consequently, not only was the separation of powers among the branches within the federal government important in preventing the centralization of power; so too was the enumeration of specific powers within each branch of the federal government and in the federal constitution generally, thereby leaving all other governing authority to the states.

The conceptual framework for federalism, or the confederation of states—where governing power is decentralized, shared, and divided among governing entities under a unified whole—predates the American founding. For example, Johannes Althusius (1563–1638), a German jurist and philosopher who provided the most elaborate exposition and defense of federalism, and who was informed by Aristotle, Cicero, and others, wrote about the early development of federalism in his book *Politica* (1603). "Even though these heads, prefects, and rectors [governors or magistrates] of provinces recognize the supreme magistrate of the realm [kingdom or nation] as their superior, from whom their administration and power are conceded, nevertheless they have rights of sovereignty in their territory, and stand in the place of the supreme prince. They prevail as much in their territory as does the emperor or supreme magistrate in the realm, except for superiority, preeminence, and certain other things specifically reserved to the supreme magistrate who does the constituting. Such is the common judgment of jurists. The head of the province therefore has the right of superiority and regal privileges in his territory, but without prejudice to the universal jurisdiction that the supreme prince has. . . ."[54] Conversely, "[t]yranny is the contrary of just and upright administration. By it the foundations and bonds of universal association are obstinately, persistently, and insanely destroyed and overthrown by the supreme magistrate against his pledged word and declared oath. . . . A tyrant is therefore one who, violating both word and oath, begins to shake the foundations and loosen the bonds of the associated body of the commonwealth. A tyrant may be either a monarch or polyarch [where power is exercised by multiple officials] that through avarice, pride, or perfidy cruelly overthrows and destroys the most important goods of the commonwealth, such as its peace, virtue, order, law, and mobility. . . ."[55]

Moreover, as University of Chicago law professor Alison L. LaCroix explains in her book, *The Ideological Origins of American Federalism* (2010), federalism in various ways was practiced in America even before the Constitution was adopted:

> [T]he history of American federalism began decades before the Constitutional Convention of 1787. Some of federalism's central concepts, most notably the idea of constructing a government around multilayered legislative authority, had begun to emerge in the 1760s and 1770s, cobbled together by members of the colonial opposition in the midst of protracted disputes between British North Americans and their metropolitan counterparts. Nevertheless, the debates at the Constitutional Convention . . . represented a vital moment in which British imperial precedents, colonial practices, postwar exigency, and political theory came together in the hands of particular individuals to form both a new idea of government and an actual new government. The

convention debates and the Constitution that resulted created and codified federalism in important ways. Arguments about the nature and scope of Parliament's power to regulate the colonies, which began as the colonists' response to what they viewed as unconstitutional legislation from Westminster, became by the 1780s a full-blown theory of government authority. With the rebellion against Britain behind them, the members of the founding generation were able—indeed, required—to consolidate the previous two decades' many shreds and pieces of structural and political argument into a more or less coherent conception of government. In this sense, then, the discussions in Philadelphia represented neither an original moment of genius nor simply another instance of negotiation among existing groups and institutions. Rather, the period from 1787 to 1789 should be understood as a reexamination and reshuffling of fundamental ideas of government which Americans had begun experimenting with decades before. The drafting and ratification of the Constitution served to crystallize a novel, distinctively British North American theory of government that had been developing since at least the mid-1760s.[56]

Again, the *Federalist Papers* are instructive. In *Federalist* 9 (November 21, 1787), Alexander Hamilton wrote:

The utility of a Confederacy, as well to suppress faction and to guard the internal tranquility of States, as to increase their external force and security, is in reality not a new idea. It has been practiced upon in different countries and ages, and has received the sanction of the most approved writers on the subject of politics. . . .

The proposed Constitution, so far from implying an abolition of the State governments, makes them constituent parts of the national sovereignty, by allowing them a direct representation in the Senate, and leaves in their possession certain exclusive and very important portions of sovereign power. This fully corresponds, in every rational import of the terms, with the idea of a federal government.[57]

In *Federalist* 32 (January 3, 1788), Hamilton wrote:

An entire consolidation of the States into one complete national sovereignty would imply an entire subordination of the parts; and whatever powers might remain in them, would be altogether dependent on the general will. But as the plan of the convention aims only at a partial union or consolidation, the State governments would clearly retain all the rights of sovereignty which they before had, and which were not, by that act, EXCLUSIVELY delegated to the United States. This exclusive delegation, or rather this alienation, of State sovereignty, would only exist in three cases: where the Constitution in express terms granted an exclusive authority to the Union; where it granted in one instance an authority to the Union, and in another prohibited the States from exercising the like authority; and where it granted an authority to the Union, to which a similar authority in the States would be absolutely and totally CONTRADICTORY and REPUGNANT.[58]

In *Federalist* 39 (January 16, 1788), Madison wrote:

The first question that offers itself is, whether the general form and aspect of the government be strictly republican. It is evident that no other form would be reconcilable with the genius of the people of America; with the fundamental principles of the Revolution; or with that honorable determination which animates every votary of freedom, to rest all our political experiments on the capacity of mankind for self-government. . . . The proposed Constitution . . . is, in strictness, neither a national nor a federal Constitution, but a composition of both. In its foundation it is federal, not national; in the sources from which the ordinary powers of the government are drawn, it is partly federal and partly national; in the operation of these powers, it is national, not federal; in the extent of them, again, it is federal, not national. . . .[59]

In *Federalist* 45 (January 26, 1788), Madison wrote:

The powers reserved to the several States will extend to all the objects which, in the ordinary course of affairs, concern the lives, liberties, and properties of the people, and the internal order, improvement, and prosperity of the State. The operations of the federal government will be most extensive and important in times of war and danger; those of the State governments, in times of peace and security. As the former periods will probably bear a small proportion to the latter, the State governments will here enjoy another advantage over the federal government. The more adequate, indeed, the federal powers may be rendered to the national defense, the less frequent will be those scenes of danger which might favor their ascendancy over the governments of the particular States. If the new Constitution be examined with accuracy and candor, it will be found that the change which it proposes consists much less in the addition of NEW POWERS to the Union, than in the invigoration of its ORIGINAL POWERS. The regulation of commerce, it is true, is a new power; but that seems to be an addition which few oppose, and from which no apprehensions are entertained. The powers relating to war and peace, armies and fleets, treaties and finance, with the other more considerable powers, are all vested in the existing Congress by the

> articles of Confederation. The proposed change does not enlarge these powers; it only substitutes a more effectual mode of administering them.[60]

In addition to the Constitution's federalist structure, the Tenth Amendment was included among the initial amendments to the Constitution, and it emphasized further the significance of federalism. Again, it reads: "The powers not delegated to the United States by the Constitution, nor prohibited by it to the states, are reserved to the states respectively, or to the people."[61]

Moreover, the spirit and character of the Constitution, its formulations and purposes, was a reflection of the nation's personality. In his book *The Roots of American Order* (1974), Russell Kirk explained:

> The true Constitution of any political state is not merely a piece of parchment, but rather a body of fundamental laws and customs that join together the various regions and classes and interests of a country, in a political pattern that is just. The English constitution is said to be "unwritten": that is, there exists no single formal document which can be called the Constitution of the United Kingdom. Certain great permanent charters, statutes, and usages, and long-accepted political conventions make up that system of practices and principles, vaguely delimited

but strong entrenched, which is British constitutional government. Similarly, even the American Republic possesses an underlying unwritten constitution—of which the written Constitution of the United States is an expression. The written Constitution has survived and has retained authority because it is in harmony with laws, customs, habits, and popular beliefs that existed before the Constitutional Convention met at Philadelphia—and which still work among Americans today. The written Constitution produced by the delegates from the several states drew upon the political experience of the colonies, upon their legacy of English law and institutions, upon the lessons of America under the Articles of Confederation, upon popular consensus about certain moral and social questions. Thus the Constitution was no abstract or utopian document, but a reflection and embodiment of political reality in America. Once ratified, the Constitution could obtain the willing compliance of most Americans because it set down formally and in practical fashion much of the "unwritten" constitution of American society.[62]

As discussed earlier, progressives find this entire governing formulation and its earlier foundational influences intolerable and therefore they have sought to eradicate and replace it. In one of his several manifestos, *Constitutional Government in the United States* (1908), Woodrow Wilson regurgitated Rousseau's theory that government and society are akin to living beings with organs that cannot function separately and apart from each other, a frequent theme among progressives promoting the centralization and concentration of power. "It is difficult to describe any single part of a great governmental system without describing the whole of it. Governments are living things and operate as organic wholes. Moreover, governments have their natural evolution and are one thing in one age, another in another. The makers of the Constitution constructed the federal government upon a theory of checks and balances which was meant to limit the operation of each part and allow to no single part or organ of it a dominating force; but no government can be successfully conducted upon so mechanical of a theory."[63]

Wilson, like other progressives of the past and present, contended that the American constitutional system is a relic, incompatible with a modern society. "The makers of our federal Constitution followed the scheme as they found it expounded by Montesquieu, followed it with genuine scientific enthusiasm. The admirable expositions of the *Federalist* read like thoughtful applications of Montesquieu to the political needs and circumstances of America. They are full of the theory of checks and balances. The President is balanced off against Congress, Congress against the President, and each against the courts. Our statesmen of the earlier generations quote no one so often as Montesquieu, and they quoted him always as a scientific standard in the field of politics. Politics is turned into mechanics under this touch. . . . The trouble with the theory is that government is not a machine, but a living thing. It falls, not under the theory of the universe, but under the theory of organic life." Wilson added: "[Government] is modified by its environment, necessitated by its tasks, shaped to its functions by sheer pressure of life. No living thing can have its organs offset against each other as checks, and live. . . . This is not theory, but fact, and displays its force as fact, whatever theories may be thrown across its track. Living political constitutions must be Darwinian [evolutionary] in structure and practice."[64]

However, the purpose of the Constitution is not to supplant or smother the civil society and in turn the free will of the individual with a powerful central government, but to safeguard them—that is, to control the rulers and uphold the society. There is nothing scientific or mechanical about it. The American founding was not an experiment in governmental extravagance but an effort to ensure that the individual can prosper in a just and stable environment. Of course, the Constitution can be modified by its amendment processes under Article V, which requires the consideration, input, and approval of a broad spectrum of the body politic. But for Wilson and the progressives, this is far too cumbersome. Law is useless if not used to empower the state and societal transformation, constitutional constraints and processes be damned.

Moreover, despite populist themes and claims of popular

will, progressives prefer domination. Obviously, centralized governmental decision making provides social engineers and planners far greater latitude to act. Consequently, the power center for Wilson and the progressive is, unsurprisingly, the executive branch.

Wilson proclaimed: "Some of our Presidents have deliberately held themselves off from using the full power they might legitimately have used, because of conscientious scruples, because they were more theorists than statesmen. They have held to the strict literary theory of the Constitution . . . and have acted as if they thought that Pennsylvania Avenue should have been even longer than it is; that there should be no intimate communication of any kind between the Capitol and the White House; that the President as a man was no more at liberty to lead the houses of Congress by persuasion than he was at liberty as President to dominate them by authority,—supposing that he had, what he has not, authority enough to dominate them. But the makers of the Constitution were not enacting Whig theory, they were not making laws with the expectation that, not the laws themselves, but their opinions, known by future historians to lie back of them, should govern the constitutional action of the country. They were statesmen, not pedants, and their laws are sufficient to keep us to the paths they set us upon. The President is at liberty, both in law and conscience, to be as big a man as he can. His capacity will set the limit; and if Congress be overborne by him, it will be no fault of the makers of the Constitution,—it will be from no lack of constitutional powers on its part, but only because the President has the nation behind him, and Congress has not."[65]

Wilson's disingenuousness is stark. He inverted the Constitution and the framers' intent to advance a theory of government that would destroy what they established and gainsay the principles they repeatedly advocated. As is all too common among progressives, Wilson exploited the language of the Constitution, which he abhorred, to justify his ideological ends. Consequently, Wilson insisted that the president best represents the people, speaks for the people, and sets the political policy agenda for the nation. The president, under Wilson's model, is a unitary voice of the government and the executive in charge of the administrative state. He can hold the rest of government accountable to the people, which, of course, is another perversion of republicanism. Unfortunately, there is little debate that this is a more accurate description of the current federal government than that which was actually established by the Constitution. Professors Bruce P. Frohnen and George W. Carey lamented that "presidents increasingly are claiming for themselves, and being accorded, the old, royal power to act outside the law so long as it is in some sense 'in the public interest.'"[66]

Indeed, Congress, which was to be a coequal branch of the federal government, if not the most important, now occupies a lesser role than the others due to its own conferral of lawmaking authority to the executive branch's administrative state or by inaction when the president seizes more legislative authority or unilaterally rules over the top of Congress. The evidence of executive legislating is overwhelming. In matters large and small, the administrative state rules. The constitutional structure has been significantly diminished. The Congressional Research Service recently reported that according to the Office of the Federal Registrar, "the number of final rules published each year [by the executive branch] is generally in the range of 2,500–4,500."[67] The Competitive Enterprise Institute determined that by December 30, 2016, in a record-setting *Federal Register* of 97,110 pages, agencies had issued 3,853 rules and regulations, 43 more than 2015 and eighteen times the number of laws (Public Laws) Congress passed during the year.[68]

| *The Unconstitutionality Index* | | | |
|---|---|---|---|
| Public Laws vs. Agency Rulemakings | | | |
| Year | Final Rules | Public Laws | THE "INDEX" |
| 2003 | 4148 | 198 | 21 |
| 2004 | 4101 | 299 | 14 |
| 2005 | 3975 | 161 | 25 |
| 2006 | 3178 | 321 | 12 |

(*continued*)

| Year | Final Rules | Public Laws | THE "INDEX" |
|---|---|---|---|
| 2007 | 3595 | 188 | 19 |
| 2008 | 3830 | 285 | 13 |
| 2009 | 3503 | 125 | 28 |
| 2010 | 3573 | 217 | 16 |
| 2011 | 3807 | 81 | 47 |
| 2012 | 3708 | 127 | 29 |
| 2013 | 3659 | 72 | 51 |
| 2014 | 3554 | 224 | 16 |
| 2015 | 3410 | 115 | 30 |
| 2016 | 3853 | 211 | 18 |

Such administrative legislating also contravenes Montesquieu's warning about the nature of lawmaking. Montesquieu explained that the promulgation of laws by republican governments must comport with the nature of the society and the government. Otherwise, a country risks decline or tyranny. He wrote: "Laws must relate to the nature and the principle of government that is established or that one wants to establish, whether those laws form it as do political laws, or maintain it, as do civil laws."[69] "There are two sorts of tyranny: a real one, which consists in the violence of the government, and one of opinion, which is felt when those who govern establish things that run counter to a nation's way of thinking."[70] "The legislator is to follow the spirit of the nation when doing so is not contrary to the principles of the government, for we do nothing better than what we do freely and by following our national genius. If one gives a pedantic spirit to a nation naturally full of gaiety, the state will gain nothing, either at home or abroad. Let it do frivolous things seriously and serious things gaily."[71]

Of course, the entire progressive enterprise is about zealously and endlessly reformulating, reconfiguring, reengineering, remaking, etc., the nature of society and the individual through a growing labyrinth of departments and agencies, and rules and decrees. There is relentless planning, programming, regulating, overseeing, etc., by the administrative state, often in contravention of the public will and without the consent of the people's representatives. All is in a state of flux and perpetual motion except, of course, the fact of the progressive ideology and agenda, which finds permanence within the Leviathan it has created.

The iconic Scottish economist and philosopher Adam Smith (1723–1790), a contemporary of the American Founders and friend of Edmund Burke, smartly diagnosed the difference between the man of true public spirit and the man of arrogance and conceit, praising the former and condemning the latter. In his acclaimed essay *The Theory of Moral Sentiments* (1759), Smith stated:

> The man whose public spirit is prompted altogether by humanity and benevolence, will respect the established

powers and privileges even of individuals, and still more those of the great orders and societies, into which the state is divided. Though he should consider some of them as in some measure abusive, he will content himself with moderating, what he often cannot annihilate without great violence. When he cannot conquer the rooted prejudices of the people by reason and persuasion, he will not attempt to subdue them by force; but will religiously observe what, by Cicero, is justly called the divine maxim of Plato, never to use violence to his country no more than to his parents. He will accommodate, as well as he can, his public arrangements to the confirmed habits and prejudices of the people; and will remedy as well as he can, the inconveniencies which may flow from the want of those regulations which the people are averse to submit to. When he cannot establish the right, he will not disdain to ameliorate the wrong; but like Solon, when he cannot establish the best system of laws, he will endeavor to establish the best that the people can bear.

The man of system, on the contrary, is apt to be very wise in his own conceit; and is often so enamored with the supposed beauty of his own ideal plan of government, that he cannot suffer the smallest deviation from any part of it. He goes on to establish it completely and in all its parts, without any regard either to the great interests, or to the strong prejudices which may oppose it. He seems to imagine that he can arrange the different members of a great society with as much ease as the hand arranges the different pieces upon a chess-board. He does not consider that the pieces upon the chess-board have no other principle of motion besides that which the hand impresses upon them; but that, in the great chess-board of human society, every single piece has a principle of motion of its own, altogether different from that which the legislature might choose to impress upon it. If those two principles coincide and act in the same direction, the game of human society will go on easily and harmoniously, and is very likely to be happy and successful. If they are opposite or different, the game will go on miserably, and the society must be at all times in the highest degree of disorder.

Some general, and even systematical, idea of the perfection of policy and law, may no doubt be necessary for directing the views of the statesman. But to insist upon establishing, and upon establishing all at once, and in spite of all opposition, everything which that idea may seem to require, must often be the highest degree of arrogance. It is to erect his own judgment into the supreme standard of right and wrong. It is to fancy himself the only wise and worthy man in the commonwealth, and that his fellow-citizens should accommodate themselves to him and not he to them. It is upon this account, that of all political speculators, sovereign princes are by far the most dangerous. This arrogance is perfectly familiar to them. They entertain no doubt of the immense superiority of their own judgment. When such imperial and royal reformers, therefore, condescend to contemplate the constitution of the country which is committed to their government, they seldom see anything so wrong in it as the obstructions which it may sometimes oppose to the execution of their own will. They hold in contempt the divine maxim of Plato, and consider the state as made for themselves, not themselves for the state. The great object of their reformation, therefore, is to remove those obstructions; to reduce the authority of the nobility; to take away the privileges of cities and provinces, and to render both the greatest individuals and the greatest orders of the state, as incapable of opposing their commands, as the weakest and most insignificant.[72]

SIX

# LIBERTY AND PROPERTY

I HAVE WRITTEN OF a humane society as ordered around natural law (including external truths and moral order), unalienable rights (including individual liberty and justice), and the institution of constitutional republicanism (including order and consent). These are among the essential doctrines and principles of the American founding. They are a function of each other and essential elements of each other. And yet, there is a remaining indivisible ingredient without which they are all imperiled—private property rights and, more broadly, what today is called market capitalism. This is a subject that pervades philosophy, including that which has been discussed throughout the book. Thus far, it has been addressed most directly but not exclusively in the context of Marx's mate-

rial historicism, but it obviously permeates the writings of the other thinkers as well.

In *Liberty and Tyranny* I explained that "[p]rivate property is the material manifestation of the individual's labor—the material value created from the intellectual and/or physical labor of the individual, which may take the form of income, real property, or intellectual property. Just as life is finite, so too is the extent of one's labor. Therefore, taxation of private property, or the regulation of such property so as to reduce its value, can become in effect a form of servitude, particularly if the dispossession results from illegitimate and arbitrary state action."[1]

In *The Second Treatise of Government*, John Locke asserted: "[The government] cannot take from any man any part of his property without his own consent. For the preservation of property being the end of government, and that for which men enter into society it necessarily supposes and requires, that the people should have property, without which they must be suppos'd to lose that by entering into society, which was the end for which they entered into it, too gross an absurdity for any man to own."[2] William Blackstone, in his *Commentaries on the Laws of England*, explained: "So great . . . is the regard of the law for private property, that it will not authorize the least violation of it; no, not even for the general good of the whole community. If a new road, for instance, were to be made through the grounds of a private person, it might perhaps be extensively beneficial to the public; but the law

permits no man, or set of them, to do this without the consent of the owner of the land."[3]

In 1787, in his essay *Defence of the Constitutions of Government of the United States*, John Adams explained the importance of protecting private property as a right from the tyranny of undiluted democracy:

> Suppose a nation, rich and poor, high and low, ten millions in number, all assembled together; not more than one or two millions will have lands, houses, or any personal property; if we take into the account the women and children, or even if we leave them out of the question, a great majority of every nation is wholly destitute of property, except a small quantity of clothes, and a few trifles of other movables. Would Mr. Nedham be responsible that, if all were to be decided by a vote of the majority, the eight or nine millions who have no property, would not think of usurping over the rights of the one or two millions who have? Property is surely a right of mankind as really as liberty. Perhaps, at first, prejudice, habit, shame or fear, principle or religion, would restrain the poor from attacking the rich, and the idle from usurping on the industrious; but the time would not be long before courage and enterprise would come, and pretexts be invented by degrees, to countenance the majority in dividing all the property among them, or at least, in sharing it equally with its present possessors. Debts would be

> abolished first; taxes laid heavy on the rich, and not at all on the others; and at last a downright equal division of every thing be demanded, and voted. What would be the consequence of this? The idle, the vicious, the intemperate, would rush into the utmost extravagance of debauchery, sell and spend all their share, and then demand a new division of those who purchased from them. The moment the idea is admitted into society, that property is not as sacred as the laws of God, and that there is not a force of law and public justice to protect it, anarchy and tyranny commence. If "Thou shalt not covet," and "Thou shalt not steal," were not commandments of Heaven, they must be made inviolable precepts in every society, before it can be civilized or made free.[4]

James Madison provided an even more comprehensive explanation about the relationship between liberty and property; that property is a right in one's self, secured for the individual and by society through constitutional republicanism. In 1792, Madison wrote:

> This term [property] in its particular application means "that dominion which one man claims and exercises over the external things of the world, in exclusion of every other individual." In its larger and juster meaning, it embraces every thing to which a man may attach a value and have a right; and *which leaves to every one else the like*

*advantage*. In the former sense, a man's land, or merchandize, or money is called his property. In the latter sense, a man has a property in his opinions and the free communication of them.

He has a property of peculiar value in his religious opinions, and in the profession and practice dictated by them. He has a property very dear to him in the safety and liberty of his person. He has an equal property in the free use of his faculties and free choice of the objects on which to employ them.

In a word, as a man is said to have a right to his property, he may be equally said to have a property in his rights. Where an excess of power prevails, property of no sort is duly respected. No man is safe in his opinions, his person, his faculties, or his possessions. Where there is an excess of liberty, the effect is the same, tho' from an opposite cause.

Government is instituted to protect property of every sort; as well that which lies in the various rights of individuals, as that which the term particularly expresses. This being the end of government, that alone is a *just* government, which *impartially* secures to every man, whatever is his *own*.

According to this standard of merit, the praise of affording a just securing to property, should be sparingly bestowed on a government which, however scrupulously guarding the possessions of individuals, does not protect them in the enjoyment and communication of their opinions, in which they have an equal, and in the estimation of some, a more valuable property.

More sparingly should this praise be allowed to a government, where a man's religious rights are violated by penalties, or fettered by tests, or taxed by a hierarchy. Conscience is the most sacred of all property; other property depending in part on positive law, the exercise of that, being a natural and unalienable right. To guard a man's house as his castle, to pay public and enforce private debts with the most exact faith, can give no title to invade a man's conscience which is more sacred than his castle, or to withhold from it that debt of protection, for which the public faith is pledged, by the very nature and original conditions of the social pact.

That is not a just government, nor is property secure under it, where the property which a man has in his personal safety and personal liberty, is violated by arbitrary seizures of one class of citizens for the service of the rest. . . .

That is not a just government, nor is property secure under it, where arbitrary restrictions, exemptions, and monopolies deny to part of its citizens that free use of their faculties, and free choice of their occupations, which not only constitute their property in the general sense of the word; but are the means of acquiring property strictly so called. What must be the spirit of legislation where a manufacturer of linen cloth is forbidden to bury his own child in a linen shroud, in order to favor his neighbor who manufactures woolen cloth; where the manufacturer and wearer of woolen cloth are again forbidden the economical use of buttons of that material, in favor of the manufacturer of buttons of other materials!

A just security to property is not afforded by that government, under which unequal taxes oppress one species of property and reward another species: where arbitrary taxes invade the domestic sanctuaries of the rich, and excessive taxes grind the faces of the poor; where the keenness and competitions of want are deemed an insufficient spur to labor, and taxes are again applied, by an unfeeling policy, as another spur; in violation of that sacred property, which Heaven, in decreeing man to earn his bread by the sweat of his brow, kindly reserved to him, in the small repose that could be spared from the supply of his necessities.

If there be a government then which prides itself in maintaining the inviolability of property; which provides that none shall be taken *directly* even for public use without indemnification to the owner, and yet *directly* violates the property which individuals have in their opinions, their religion, their persons, and their faculties; nay more, which *indirectly* violates their property, in their actual possessions, in the labor that acquires their daily subsistence, and in the hallowed remnant of time which ought to re-

> lieve their fatigues and soothe their cares, the influence will have been anticipated, that such a government is not a pattern for the United States.
>
> If the United States mean to obtain or deserve the full praise due to wise and just governments, they will equally respect the rights of property, and the property in rights: they will rival the government that most sacredly guards the former; and by repelling its example in violating the latter, will make themselves a pattern to that and all other governments.[5]

In "one's self" Madison was speaking of individualism and the individual's unalienable rights, of which property per se and property in its broader context are both consequential and imperative. In fact, it is impossible to delink the principle of property rights from individual rights and liberty generally.

F. A. Hayek noted the distinctions between the two kinds of individualism addressed earlier in this book—that is, the real individualism associated with individual liberty and the so-called individualism hawked by philosophers like Rousseau and modern progressives, in which the individual is contorted and subsumed by the collective. In his book *Individualism and Economic Order* (1949), Hayek explained that "while the design theories necessarily lead to the conclusion that social processes can be made to serve human ends only if they are subjected to the control of individual human reason, and thus lead directly to socialism, true individualism believes on the contrary that, if left free, men will often achieve more than individual human reason could design or foresee. This contrast between the true, antirationalistic and the false, rationalistic individualism permeates all social thought. But because both theories have become known by the same name . . . all sorts of conceptions and assumptions completely alien to true individualism have come to be regarded as essential parts of its doctrine."[6]

Like Adams, Hayek argued that rather than freeing the individual, the scientism, historicism, and progressivism of those who seek to redesign society cannot possibly succeed in producing an economic utopia, no matter how smart the masterminds may be or think they are. "[I]t is an indisputable intellectual fact which nobody can hope to alter . . . [that is,] the constitutional limitation of man's knowledge and interests, the fact that he cannot know more than a tiny part of the whole of society and that therefore all that can enter into his motives are the immediate effects which his actions will have in the sphere he knows."[7]

Moreover, individual liberty is impossible if the governing goal is the pursuit of economic egalitarianism and social sameness. Individuals are unique in myriad ways. For the Founders, equality meant equal justice and equality under the law, not the uniformity of men and conformity to centralized plans and rules. Hayek explained: "[O]nly because men are in fact unequal can we treat them equally. If all men were completely equal in their gifts and inclinations, we should have to treat them differently in order to achieve any sort of social organization. Fortunately, they are not equal; and it is only owing to this that the differentiation of functions need not be determined by the arbitrary decision of some organizing will but that, after creating formal equality of the rules applying in the same manner to all, we can leave each individual to find his own level. There is all the difference in the world between treating people equally and attempting to make them equal. . . ."[8]

Therefore, as Madison, Adams, and the other Founders universally understood, the individual can best exercise and enjoy his unalienable rights, and the civil society is best preserved if not improved, through a constitution that establishes a republican form of governance with distinct limits and boundaries. Hayek explained: "While the theory of individualism has thus a definite contribution to make to the technique of constructing a suitable legal framework and of improving the institutions which have grown up spontaneously, its emphasis . . . is on the fact that the part of our social order which can or ought to be made a conscious product of human reason is only a small part of all the forces of society. . . ."[9]

Hayek also wrote that unrestrained "democracy" or majority rule or populism can descend into mobocracy, anarchy, and, ultimately, some form of tyranny. "There are two more points of difference between the two kinds of individualism which are also best illustrated by the stand taken by Lord Acton and de Tocqueville by their view on democracy and equality towards trends which become prominent in their time. True individualism not only believes in democracy but can claim that democratic ideals spring from the basic principles of individualism. Yet, while individualism affirms that all government should be democratic, it has no superstitious belief in the omnicompetence of majority decisions, and in particular it refuses to admit that 'absolute power may, by the hypothesis of popular origin, be as legitimate as constitutional freedom.' It believes that under a democracy, no less than under any other form of government, 'the sphere of enforced command ought to be restricted within fixed limits'; and it is particularly opposed to the most fateful and dangerous of all current misconceptions of democracy—the belief that we must accept as true and binding for future development the views of the majority. While democracy is founded on the convention that the majority view decides on common action, it does not mean that what is today the majority view ought to become the generally accepted view—even if that were necessary to achieve the aims of the majority. On the contrary, the whole justification of democracy rests on the fact that in course of time what is today the view of a small minority may become the majority view. . . ."[10]

Hayek condemned the progressive ideology as intellectually supercilious, economically destructive, and factually impossible. Furthermore, he feared that once it took hold in a society, it might become impossible to reverse course. "The unwillingness to tolerate or respect any social forces which are not recognizable as the product of intelligent design, which is so important a cause of the present desire for comprehensive economic planning, is indeed only one aspect of a more general movement. We meet the same tendency in the field of morals and conventions, in the desire to substitute an artificial for the existing languages, and in the whole modern attitude toward processes which govern the growth of knowledge. The belief that only a synthetic system of morals, an artificial language, or even an artificial society can be justified in an age of science, as well as the increasing unwillingness to bow before any moral rules whose utility is not rationally demonstrated, or to conform with conventions whose rationale is not known, are all manifestations of the same basic view which wants all social activity to be recognizably part of a single coherent plan. They are the results of the same rationalistic 'individualism' which wants to see in everything the product of a conscious individual reason. They are certainly not, however, a result of true individualism and may even make the working of a free and truly individualist system difficult or impossible." Hayek then warned: "Indeed, the great lesson which the individualist philosophy teaches us on this score is that, while it may not be difficult to destroy the spontaneous formations which are the indispensable bases of a free civilization, it may be beyond our power deliberately to reconstruct such a civilization once these foundations are destroyed."[11]

Does this mean there should be no occasion for governmental intervention? Of course not. However, as discussed earlier in relation to negative and positive liberty, there is intervention for the purpose of domination and state expansion, and intervention for the purpose of securing true individualism and proper order. This would also apply to certain economic considerations and conditions, such as the vitality of market competition.

Hayek argued: "It is important not to confuse opposition against this kind of [scientific] planning with a dogmatic laissez faire attitude. The [classical] liberal argument in favor of making the best possible use of the forces of competition as a means of coordinating human efforts, is not an argument for leaving things just as they are. It is based on the conviction that, where effective competition can be created, it is a better way of guiding individual efforts than any other. It does not deny, but even emphasizes, that, in order that competition should work beneficially, a carefully thought-out legal framework is required and that neither the existing nor the past legal rules are free from grave defects. Nor does it deny that, where it is impossible to create the conditions necessary to make competition effective, we must resort to other methods of guiding economic activity. Economic liberalism is opposed, however, to competition being supplanted by inferior methods of coordinating individual efforts. And it regards competition as superior not only because it is in most circumstances the most efficient method known but even more because it is the only method by which our activities can be adjusted to each other without coercive or arbitrary intervention of authority.

Indeed, one of the main arguments in favor of competition is that it dispenses with the need for 'conscious social control' and that it gives the individual a chance to decide whether the prospects of a particular occupation are sufficient to compensate for the disadvantages and risks connected with it."[12]

Hence, governing regulations informed by America's founding principles and instituted for the limited but significant purpose of nurturing, improving, or promoting private property and economic vibrancy are both prudential and essential to safeguarding individual liberty and the civil society. However, regulations that have as their purpose the institution of plans and schemes to fundamentally transform society in ways that extinguish "the spirit of the nation"—and are motivated by the progressive ideology, special interests, crony capitalism, etc.—are a perversion and abuse of legitimate governing authority. "To create conditions in which competition will be as effective as possible," wrote Hayek, "to supplement it where it cannot be made effective, to provide the services which, in the words of Adam Smith, 'though they may be in the highest degree advantageous to a great society, are, however, of such a nature, that the profit could never repay the expense to any individual or small number of individuals'—these tasks provide, indeed, a wide and unquestioned field for state activity. In no system that could be rationally defended would the state just do nothing. An effective competitive system needs an intelligently designed and continuously adjusted legal framework as much as any other. Even the most essential prerequisite of its proper functioning, the prevention of fraud and deception . . . provides a great and by no means yet fully accomplished object of legislative activity."[13]

Underscoring Hayek's point about "promoting the forces of competition," it is well to remember that the precursor to the Constitutional Convention of 1787 in Philadelphia was the Annapolis Convention in September 1786, the focus of which was the devastating protectionist trade barriers the states were imposing on each other, thereby interfering with interstate trade and competition. Twelve delegates from five states convened. As was later reported, "That, pursuant to their several appointments, they met, at Annapolis in the State of Maryland on the eleventh day of September Instant, and having proceeded to a Communication of their Powers; they found that the States of New York, Pennsylvania, and Virginia, had, in substance, and nearly in the same terms, authorized their respective Commissions 'to meet such other Commissioners as were, or might be, appointed by the other States in the Union, at such time and place as should be agreed upon by the said Commissions to take into consideration the trade and commerce of the United States, to consider how far a uniform system in their commercial intercourse and regulations might be necessary to their common interest and permanent harmony, and to report to the several States such an Act, relative to this great object, as when unanimously by them would enable the United States in Congress assembled effectually to provide for the same. . . .'"[14]

Little came of the Annapolis Convention. But the states

knew they had to tackle the commerce and trade problem or else the nation would face potential ruin. As Supreme Court associate justice Joseph Story would later write about the nation's economy: "It is hardly possible to exaggerate the oppressed and degraded state of domestic commerce, manufactures, and agriculture, at the time of the adoption of the Constitution. Our ships were almost driven from the ocean; our work-shops were nearly deserted; our mechanics were in a starving condition; and our agriculture was sunk to the lowest ebb. These were the natural results of the inability of the General Government to regulate commerce, so as to prevent the injurious [state] monopolies and exclusions of foreign nations, and the conflicting, and often ruinous regulations of the different states."[15]

The states agreed to a subsequent convention, this time in Philadelphia—the Constitutional Convention. The matter of interstate commerce would be specifically addressed in Article I, Section 8, Clause 1 of the Constitution. It provides, in part, that Congress shall have power "[t]o regulate Commerce with foreign Nations, and among the several States, and with the Indian Tribes."[16] Obviously, the purpose of the clause was to encourage commerce—that is, property rights and market capitalism. The Commerce Clause was the method by which the Framers balanced, among other things, federalism with economic liberty, particularly property rights. However, the progressives distorted the Commerce Clause, like much of the rest of the Constitution, and have interpreted it to mean the opposite of what was intended. Rather than promoting interstate commerce, the clause has been used to empower the centralized administrative state and its regulatory ambitions, both interstate and intrastate; it has been turned against the object of its protection—private property rights and market capitalism. Thus much of what the administrative does is without constitutional authority, judicial pronouncements and imprimaturs to the contrary.

In 1996, in a law review article titled "Judicial Manipulation of the Commerce Clause," eminent Harvard Law Professor and constitutional scholar Raoul Berger (1901–2000) found absolutely no justification for much of the administrative state's modern-day regulatory activity. "The Founders' all-but-exclusive concern was with exactions by some states from their neighbors. [James] Madison said, 'It would be unjust to the States whose produce was exported by their neighbours, to leave it subject to be taxed by the latter.' [James] Wilson 'dwelt on the injustice and impolicy of leaving New Jersey[,] Connecticut &c and longer subject to the exactions of their commercial neighbours.' That the Commerce Clause was meant to remedy this mischief is clear. Madison stated that it was necessary to remove 'existing & injurious retaliations *among* the States,' that 'the best guard against [this 'abuse'] was the right in the Genl. Government to regulate trade *between* State and State.' [Roger] Sherman stated that 'the oppression of the uncommercial States was guarded agst. by the power to regulate trade between the States.' And Oliver Elseworth said that the 'power of regulating trade between the States will protect them agst each other.' Given the jealous attachment to state sovereignty, the absence of objection that the Commerce Clause invaded State autonomy indicates that such an intrusion [by the federal government into intrastate economic activity] was simply unimaginable. [Thomas] Jefferson accurately reflected the Founders' views when he stated in 1791 that 'the power given to Congress by the Constitution does not extend to the internal regulation of the commerce of a state . . . which remains exclusively with its own legislature; but to its external commerce only, that is to say, its commerce with another state, or with foreign nations. . . .' That no more was intended was made clear by Madison in a letter to J. C. Cabell: '*among* the several States' . . . grew out of the abuses of the power by the importing States in taxing the non-importing, and was intended as a negative and preventive provision against injustice among the States themselves, rather than as a power to be used for the positive purposes of the General Government. . . ."[17]

In their 2013 treatise "'To Regulate,' not 'To Prohibit': Limiting the Commerce Power," Professors Barry Friedman and Genevieve Lakier also examined the history of the Commerce Clause and drew the same conclusions as Berger. "The Framers plainly sought to take from the states the power to pass 'interfering and unneighbourly regulations' of this kind. They sought to empower Congress to make uniform rules for trade. . . . The ultimate aim was to facilitate what Alexander

Hamilton described in *Federalist* 11 as the 'unrestrained intercourse between the States' that he, and other Federalists, believed would promote both economic prosperity and political unity. No one suggested, during the framing or ratification of the Constitution, that in addition to facilitating an unrestrained intercourse between the states, Congress also would be empowered to *restrain* such intercourse, by restricting what goods could cross state lines or be sold in interstate markets. When delegates referred to Congress's interstate commerce powers, they referred to them exclusively as a solution to the problem of burdensome or discriminatory state legislation. . . . In short, both positive and negative evidence suggests that the Framers did not intend—and probably did not even imagine—that the Interstate Commerce Clause would be read in such a way as to give Congress the power to restrain interstate intercourse, as well as to promote it."[18]

Again, this is also important because of the indisputable relationship between political and economic liberty, and the federal government's excessive and obsessive interference with both. Milton Friedman (1912–2006), a Nobel laureate in economics and perhaps the most prominent free market economist of the twentieth century, explained in his popular book *Capitalism and Freedom* that "[e]conomic arrangements play a dual role in the promotion of a free society. One the one hand, freedom in economic arrangements is itself a component of freedom broadly understood, so economic freedom is also an indispensable means toward the achievement of political freedom. . . . Viewed as a means to the end of political freedom, economic arrangements are important because of their effect on the concentration and dispersion of power. The kind of economic organization that provides economic freedom directly, namely, competitive capitalism, also promotes political freedom because it separates economic power from political power and in this way enables the one to offset the other." "Because we live in a largely free society, we tend to forget how limited is the span of time and the part of the globe for which there has ever been anything like political freedom: the typical state of mankind is tyranny, servitude, and misery. The nineteenth century and early twentieth century in the Western world stand out as striking exceptions to the general trend of historical development. Political freedom in this instance clearly came along with the free market and the development of capitalist institutions. So also did political freedom in the golden age of Greece and in the early days of the Roman era. History suggests only that capitalism is a necessary condition of political freedom. Clearly it is not a sufficient condition."[19]

Moreover, as progressivism's grip on society is increasingly tightened through centralized decision making, it not only induces adverse economic consequences but is also destructive of the harmony that exists among a diverse and free people in the civil society, creating balkanization and disruption. While acknowledging that absolute freedom is obviously impossible, Friedman wrote: "The use of political channels, while inevitable, tends to strain the social cohesion essential for a stable society. The strain is least if agreement for joint action need be reached only on a limited range of issues on which people in any event have common views. Every extension of the range of issues for which explicit [political] agreement is sought strains further the delicate threads that hold society together. If it goes so far as to touch an issue on which men feel deeply yet differently, it may well disrupt the society. . . . The widespread use of the market reduces the strain on the social fabric by rendering conformity unnecessary with respect to any activities it encompasses. The wider the range of activities covered by the market, the fewer are the issues on which explicitly political decisions are required and hence on which it is necessary to achieve agreement. In turn, the fewer the issues on which agreement is necessary, the greater is the likelihood of getting agreement while maintaining a free society."[20]

Friedman noted that the early progressives were persuasive because their appeals were anchored in promises of a utopian ideal, unbridled by real-world experience or reality. He wrote: "In the 1920's and the 1930's, intellectuals in the United States were overwhelmingly persuaded that capitalism was a defective system inhibiting economic well-being and thereby freedom, and that the hope for the future lay in a greater measure of deliberate control by political authorities over economic affairs. The conversion of the intellectuals was not achieved by the example of any actual collectivist society, though it undoubtedly was much hastened by the establishment of a communist society in Russia and the glowing hopes placed in it. The conversion of the intellectuals was achieved by a comparison between the existing state of affairs, with all its injustices and defects, and a hypothetical state of affairs as it might be. The actual was compared to the ideal. At the time, not much else was possible. True, mankind had experienced many epochs of centralized control, of detailed intervention by the state into economic affairs. But there had been a revolution in politics, in science, and in technology. Surely, it was argued, we can do far better with a democratic political structure, modern tools, and modern science than was possible in earlier ages."[21]

Like Hayek, Friedman acknowledged that there is an appropriate role for government and that there have been certain economic benefits from governmental intrusion—highways, dams, antitrust, public health and safety, access to education, etc. However, Friedman argued that considering the extent of government intervention and the enormous financial costs and economic dislocations, these benefits are more the exception than the rule. Friedman explained: "We now have several decades of experience with governmental intervention. It is no longer necessary to compare the market as it actually operates and government intervention as it ideally might operate. We can compare the actual with the actual. If we do so, it is clear that the difference between the actual operation of the market and its ideal operation—great though it undoubtedly is—is as nothing compared to the difference between the actual effects of government intervention and their intended effects. . . ."[22]

As I wrote in *Liberty and Tyranny*, because of its sweeping break from our founding principles and constitutional limits, the federal government has become a "massive, unaccountable conglomerate: It is the nation's largest creditor, debtor, lender, employer, consumer, contractor, grantor, property owner, tenant, insurer, health-care provider, pension, and guarantor."[23] Furthermore, in *Plunder and Deceit*, I provide extensive evidence of the economic calamity that awaits future generations as a result of the federal government's reckless extravagance and profligacy, including its more than $200 *trillion* fiscal gap.[24]

Conversely, not enough is said about the seismic benefits to individuals and society generally from private property rights, market capitalism, and the industrial revolution of the 1800s. Rather, a long list of myths intended to promote the progressive agenda has been successfully embedded in the public psyche. For example, it is said that capitalism and in particular the industrial revolution gave rise to child labor. In fact, child labor existed long before the industrial revolution—since the beginning of mankind. What of monopolies and oligopolies? Again, concentrations of economic power existed in agrarian and feudal systems and exist today under various forms of collectivism, such as socialist and communist regimes. The New Deal in the 1930s and 1940s instituted the most far-reaching and intrusive centralized management and control of private economic and business activities America had ever known. And it remains the model for government intrusion in the economy today despite its abundant demonstrable failures.

Despite its significance to the progressive enterprise, it is not possible to comprehensively tackle the New Deal in these pages. However, valuable insight is available in the book *FDR's Folly* (2003), by historian and Cato Institute senior fellow Jim Powell, and in *The Forgotten Man* (2007), by author and columnist Amity Shlaes. They provide compelling evidence of the federal government's role in exacerbating the economic conditions leading up to the Great Depression and the disastrous effects on farmers, corporations, prices, and employment.[25]

In addition, in several of the most thoroughly researched examinations of New Deal economic policies, Professors Harold L. Cole and Lee E. Ohanian supply overwhelming proof of the New Deal's deleterious effects on the economy, which both deepened and extended the Great Depression. They summarized their findings in 2009:

> The New Deal is widely perceived to have ended the Great Depression . . . But the facts do not support the perception . . . [T]here was even less work on average during the New Deal than before FDR took office. Total hours worked per adult, including government employees, were 18% below their 1929 level between 1930–32, but were 23% lower on average during the New Deal

(1933–39). Private hours worked were even lower after FDR took office, averaging 27% below their 1929 level, compared to 18% lower between in 1930–32.

Cole and Ohanian explained that it was the New Deal that actually prevented a more rapid recovery:

> The economic fundamentals that drive all expansions were very favorable during the New Deal. Productivity grew very rapidly after 1933, the price level was stable, real interest rates were low, and liquidity was plentiful. We have calculated on the basis of just productivity growth that employment and investment should have been back to normal levels by 1936 . . .
>
> Some New Deal policies certainly benefited the economy by establishing a basic social safety net . . . [b]ut others violated the most basic economic principles by suppressing competition, and setting prices and wages in many sectors well above their normal levels . . .
>
> The most damaging policies were those at the heart of the recovery plan, including The National Industrial Recovery Act (NIRA), which tossed aside the nation's antitrust acts and permitted industries to collusively raise prices provided that they shared their newfound monopoly rents with workers by substantially raising wages well above underlying productivity growth . . . Each industry created a code of "fair competition" which spelled out

what producers could and could not do, and which were designed to eliminate "excessive competition" that FDR believed to be the source of the Depression. . . .[26]

Cole and Ohanian concluded that "wholesale government intervention can—and does—deliver the most unintended consequences."

Friedman also extensively studied the causes of the Great Depression. He concluded: "The fact is that the Great Depression, like most other periods of severe unemployment, was produced by government mismanagement rather than by any inherent instability of the private economy. A governmentally established agency—the Federal Reserve System—had been assigned the responsibility for monetary policy. In 1930 and 1931, it exercised this responsibility so ineptly as to convert what otherwise would have been a moderate contraction into a major catastrophe."[27] Friedman found "that the severity of each of the major [post–World War I] contractions—1920–21, 1929–33, and 1937–38—is directly attributable to acts of commission and omission by the Reserve authorities and would not have occurred under earlier monetary and banking arrangements. There might well have been recessions on these or other occasions, but it is highly unlikely that any would have developed into a major contraction."[28] "The Great Depression . . . , far from being a sign of the inherent instability of the private enterprise system, is a testament to how much harm can be done by mistakes on the part of a few men

when they wield vast power over the monetary system of a country."[29]

Oppositely, the spectacular economic advancement that was unleashed by the industrial revolution and continues to this day, and which has massively increased the quality of life for ordinary Americans, is subjected to the progressive's constant torrent of criticism and negative charges. Therefore, a brief defense is compelled—although one would think it is unnecessary inasmuch as Americans are surrounded by and benefit from its infinite wonders.

In his book *Lectures on Economic Growth* (2004), Nobel laureate in economics and University of Chicago professor Robert E. Lucas Jr. argues that the industrial revolution was the most miraculous improvement of the standard of living and economic progress the world has ever known. "From the earliest historical times until around the beginning of the nineteenth century, the number of people in the world and the volume of goods and services they produced grew at roughly equal, slowly increasing rates. The living standards of ordinary people in eighteenth-century Europe were about the same as those of people in contemporary China or ancient Rome or, indeed, as those of people in the poorest countries in the world today. Then, during the last 200 years, both production and population growth have accelerated dramatically, and production has begun to grow *much* more rapidly than population. For the first time in history, the living standards of masses of ordinary people have begun to undergo sustained growth.

The novelty of the discovery that a human society has this potential for generating sustained improvement in the material aspects of the lives of all of its members, not just of a ruling elite, cannot be overstressed. We have entered an entirely new phase in our economic history."[30]

In his essay "An Audacious Promise: The Moral Case for Capitalism" (2012), Yeshiva University professor James R. Otteson explains: "Since 1800, the world's population has increased sixfold; yet despite this enormous increase, real income per person has increased approximately 16-fold. . . . In America, the increase is even more dramatic: in 1800, the total population in America was 5.3 million, life expectancy was 39, and the real gross domestic product per capita was $1,343 (in 2010 dollars); in 2011, our population was 308 million, our life expectancy was 78, and our GDP was $48,800. Thus even while the population increased 58-fold, our life expectancy doubled, and our GDP per capita increased almost 36-fold. Such growth is unprecedented in the history of humankind. Considering the worldwide per-capita real income for the previous 99.9 percent of human existence averaged consistently around $1 per day. That is extraordinary. What explains it? It would seem that it is due principally to the complex of institutions usually included under the term 'capitalism,' since the main thing that changed between 200 years ago and the previous 100,000 years of human history was the introduction and embrace of so-called capitalist institutions—particularly, private property and markets. One central promise of capitalism has been that it will lead to increasing material prosperity. . . ."[31]

As I argued in *Liberty and Tyranny*, "[t]he free market is the most transformative of economic systems. It fosters creativity and inventiveness. It produces new industries, products, and services, as it improves upon existing ones. With millions of individuals freely engaged in an infinite number and variety of transactions each day, it is impossible to even conceive all the changes and plans for changes occurring in our economy at any given time. The free market creates more wealth and opportunities for more people than any other economic model."[32]

For the progressive, of course, this is a dire problem. Participatory republicanism and participatory market capitalism empower the individual and improve society. Despite the radical egalitarian and class-warfare attacks of the progressives condemning capitalism as serving mostly the interests of the wealthy and promoting income inequality and social injustice, economist George Reisman, in his treatise on economics, *Capitalism* (1996), succinctly builds an overwhelming case for its universal benefits:

> Industrial civilization has radically increased life expectancy: from about thirty years in the mid-eighteenth century to about seventy-five years today. In the twen-

tieth century, in the United States, it has increased life expectancy from about forty-six years in 1900 to the present seventy-five years. The enormous contribution of industrial civilization to human life is further illustrated by the fact that the average newborn American child has a greater chance of living to age sixty-five than the average newborn child of a nonindustrial society has of living to age five. The marvelous results have come about because of an ever improving supply of food, clothing, shelter, medical care, and all the conveniences of life, and the progressive reduction in human fatigue and exhaustion. All of this has taken place on a foundation of [actual] science, technology, and capitalism, which have made possible the continuous development and introduction of new and improved products and more efficient methods of production.

In the last two centuries, loyalty to the values of science, technology, and capitalism has enabled man in the industrialized countries of the Western world to put an end to famines and plagues, and to eliminate the once dreaded diseases of cholera, diphtheria, smallpox, tuberculosis, and typhoid fever, among others. Famine has been ended, because industrial civilization has produced the greatest abundance and variety of food in the history of the world, and has created the storage and transportation systems required to bring it to everyone. This same industrial civilization has produced the greatest abundance of clothing and shoes, and of housing, in the history of the world. And while some people in the industrialized countries may be hungry or homeless . . . it is certain that no one in the industrialized countries needs to be hungry or homeless. Industrial civilization has also produced the iron and steel pipe, the chemical purification and pumping systems, and the boilers, that enable everyone to have instant access to safe drinking water, hot or cold, every minute of the day. It has produced the sewage systems and the automobiles that have removed filth of human and animal waste from the streets of cities and towns. It has produced the vaccines, anesthesias, antibiotics, and all the other "wonder drugs" of modern times, along with all kinds of new and improved diagnostic and surgical equipment. It is such accomplishments in the foundations of public health and in medicine, along with improved nutrition, clothing, and shelter, that have put an end to plagues and radically reduced the incident of almost every type of disease.

As a result of industrialized civilization, not only do billions more people survive, but in the advanced countries they do so on a level far exceeding that of kings and emperors in all previous ages—on a level that just a few generations ago would have been regarded as possible only in a world of science fiction. With the turn of a key, the push of a pedal, and the touch of a steering wheel, they drive along highways in wondrous machines at sixty miles an hour. With the flick of a switch, they light a room in the middle of darkness. With the touch of a button, they watch events taking place ten thousand miles away. With the touch of a few other buttons, they talk to other people across town or across the world. They even fly through the air at six hundred miles per hour, forty thousand feet up, watching movies and sipping martinis in air-conditioned comfort as they do so. In the United States, most people can have all this, and spacious homes or apartments, carpeted and fully furnished, with indoor plumbing, central heating, air conditioning, refrigerators, freezers, and gas or electric stoves, and also personal libraries of hundreds of books, records, compact disks, and tape recordings; they can have all this, as well as long life and good health—as the result of working forty hours a week.

The achievement of this marvelous state of affairs has been made possible by the use of ever improved machinery and equipment, which has been the focal point of scientific and technological progress. The use of this ever improved machinery and equipment is what has enabled human beings to accomplish ever greater results with the application of less and less muscular exertion.[33]

Lucas observes that the key to economic growth and prosperity, and the remarkable technological and other advances that have improved the human condition, was the recognition and legal protection of private property rights. "[T]he industrial revolution was not exclusively, or even primarily, a technological event. Important changes in technology have occurred throughout history, yet the sustained growth in living standards is an event of the last 200 years. The invention of agriculture, the domestication of animals, the invention of language, writing, mathematics, and printing, the utilization of the power of fire, wind, and water, all led to major improvements in the ability to produce enormous growth in population. Depending on where such inventions occurred, some of them induced important shifts in the relative power of different societies. By the seventeenth century, indeed, their ability to generate new technology had enabled the Europeans to conquer much of the world. Yet none of these inventions led to *any* substantial increase in the living standards of ordinary people, Europeans or otherwise. . . . Of course this is not to say that prior to the last two centuries everyone lived at a level of subsistence. . . . Wherever property rights in land and other resources have been established, property owners have enjoyed incomes in excess of, often far in excess of, subsistence."[34]

Hernando de Soto, a Peruvian economist and president of the Institute for Liberty and Democracy, agrees with Lucas but goes a step further. He explains in his book *The Mystery of Capital: Why Capitalism Triumphs in the West and Fails Everywhere Else* (2000) that property rights means more than ownership. The property holder must have the legal ability to protect his ownership right and to use his property to generate economic activity, including the creation of capital, which leads to further investments and economic growth. "In the West . . . every parcel of land, every building, every piece of equipment, or store of inventories is represented in a property document that is the visible sign of a vast hidden process that connects all these assets to the rest of the economy. Thanks to this representational process, assets can lead an invisible, parallel life alongside their material existence. They can be used as collateral for credit. The single most important source of funds for new businesses in the United States is a mortgage on the entrepreneur's house. These assets can also provide a link to the owner's credit history, an accountable address for the collection of debts and taxes, the basis for the creation of reliable and universal public utilities, and the foundation for the creation of securities (like mortgage-backed bonds) that can then be rediscounted and sold in secondary markets. By this process the West injects life into assets that makes them generate capital. Third World and former communist nations do not have this representational process. As a result, most of them are undercapitalized, in the same way that a firm is undercapitalized when it issues fewer securities than its income and assets would justify. The enterprises of the poor are very much like corporations that cannot issue shares or bonds to obtain new investment and finance. Without representations, their assets are dead capital. This is the mystery of capital. Solving it requires an understanding of why Westerners, by representing assets with titles, are able to see and draw out capital from them. One of the greatest challenges to the human mind is to comprehend and to gain access to those things we know exist but cannot see. . . ."[35]

De Soto observes that "[t]he absence of this process in the poorer regions of the world—where two-thirds of humanity live—is not the consequence of some Western monopolistic conspiracy. It is rather that they have lost all awareness of its existence. Although it is huge, nobody sees it, including the Americans, Europeans, and Japanese, who owe all their wealth to their ability to use it. It is an implicit legal infrastructure hidden deep within their property systems—of which ownership is but the tip of the iceberg. The rest of the iceberg is an intricate man-made process that can transform assets and labor into capital. This process was not created from a blueprint and it is not described in a glossy brochure. Its origins are obscure and its significance buried in the economic subconscious of Western capitalist nations."[36]

While all these superb thinkers are surely right, even more critical to understanding the American economic revolution, including the industrial revolution, is the extent of the integration and confluence of natural law principles, including unalienable rights and an eternal moral order, the evolution of the civil society, and the application of republicanism to a constitutional governing structure; and the weaving of private property rights, including commerce, trade, and mobility, into the fabric of society and institutionalized in the law. This extraordinary intertwining and aggregation of events is an essential character of the American republic. It has led to an explosion of individual ingenuity and productivity, and a fantastic quality of life for the broadest population of Americans, the likes of which the world has never before experienced.

Moreover, these confluences strengthen the character and well-being of a nation. In *The Spirit of the Laws*, Montesquieu wrote of the role of commerce in a civil society. He explained that "the spirit of commerce brings with it the spirit of frugality, economy, moderation, work, wisdom, tranquility, order, and rule. . . ."[37] "Commerce cures destructive prejudices, and it is an almost general rule that everywhere there are gentle mores, there is commerce and that everywhere there is commerce, there are gentle mores. . . ."[38] "In short, one's belief that one's prosperity is more certain in these states makes one undertake everything, and because one believes that what one has acquired is secure, one dares to expose it in order to acquire more; only the means for acquisition are at risk; now, men expect much of their future. . . . As for the despotic states, it is useless to talk about it. General rule: in a nation that is in servitude, one works more to preserve than to acquire; in a free nation, one works more to acquire that to preserve."[39]

What of society's poor? Montesquieu wrote of two kinds of poor, those who live a hopeless existence under authoritarian rule and those for whom opportunity exists in a free society. "There are two sorts of poor peoples: some are made so by the harshness of the government, and these people are capable of almost no virtue because their poverty is part of their servitude; the others are poor only because they have disdained or because they did not know the comforts of life, and these last can do great things because this poverty is part of their liberty."[40] Indeed, commerce promotes individual and societal industriousness, improvement, and progress. "Men, by their care and their good laws, have made the earth more fit to be their home. We see rivers flowing where there were lakes and marshes; it is a good that nature did not make, but which is maintained by nature. When the Persians were the masters of Asia, they permitted those who diverted the water from its source to a place that had not yet been watered to enjoy it for five generations, and, as many streams flow from the Taurus mountains, they spared no expense in getting water from there. Today, one finds it in one's fields and gardens without knowing where it comes from. Thus, just as destructive nations do evil things that last longer than themselves, there are industrious nations that do good things that do not end with themselves."[41] And commerce is natural to man and a natural characteristic of republican government. "Commerce is related to the constitution. In government by one alone, it is ordinarily founded on luxury, and though it is also founded on real needs, its principal object is to procure for the nation engaging in it all that serves its arrogance, its delights, and its fancies. In government by many, it is more often founded on economy. Traders, eyeing all the nations of earth, take to one what they bring from another. . . ."[42]

A vibrant economy and healthy society, where the people are generally productive, satisfied, and happy, is a society upon which voluntary or willing societal transformation becomes more difficult. The people, or Marx's "proletariat" working class, are actually invested in such a society because they helped build it and enjoy a higher standard of living than most. They will not rise up to lead a revolution against their best interests and to empower politicians and bureaucrats. But the progressive has decided in advance that societal transformation is necessary. Therefore he must employ various forms of usurpation and subterfuge to stir discontent and balkanize the citizenry (race, gender, income, age, religion, etc.). The individual's imperfections and the imperfections of republican institutions must be exploited, and visions of the perfect society, albeit impossible, supposedly guaranteed by the progressive's enterprise, must be propped up. The future is always said to be better than the present, but only if the individual surrenders more of his liberty and property to the state and conforms to the demands of the state. Ultimately, if persuasion by exploitation and propaganda is ineffective, the citizenry must be forced to bend to the progressive's plans by the might of government's extraconstitutional administrative means.

The philosopher Karl Popper wrote in *The Poverty of Historicism* (1957) that the human factor must be controlled "by institutional means, and to extend his program so as to embrace not only the transformation of society . . . but also the transformation of man. The political problem, therefore, is to organize human impulses in such a way that they will direct their energy to the right strategic points, and steer the total process of development in the desired direction. It seems to escape the well-meaning Utopianist that his program implies an admission of failure, even before he launches. For it substitutes for his demand that we build a new society, fit for men and women to live in, the demand that we 'mould' these men and women to fit into the new society."[43]

# EPILOGUE

IN THIS BOOK, EVEN more than my previous books, I have introduced or reintroduced the reader to numerous consequential thinkers in an effort to rekindle a love for the legacy and principles that define Americanism and a comprehension of the perils the nation faces. Much territory has been covered—philosophy, history, economics, government, and culture—making an abbreviated restatement of the previous pages impossible.

Suffice to say that America's founding principles are eternal principles. They are principles that instruct humanity today and tomorrow, as they did yesterday. These principles are born of intuition, faith, experience, and right reason. They are the foundation on which the civil society is built and the individual is cherished; they are the basis of freedom, moral order, happiness, and prosperity.

Yet these principles are apparently so grievous and abhorrent that they are mostly ignored or even ridiculed today by academia, the media, and politicians—that is, the ruling elite and its surrogates. They reject history's lessons and instead are absorbed with their own conceit and aggrandizement in the relentless pursuit of a diabolical project, the final outcome of which is an oppression of mind and soul. Indeed, our ears are pierced with the shrill and constant chorus of promises and shibboleths about utopian statism, which, of course, serve the purposes of a sterile, scientific project and its centralized administrative-state masterminds. The equality they envision, but dare not honestly proclaim, is life on the hamster wheel, where one individual is indistinguishable from the next.

In many respects, the progressive has succeeded in his primary objective: the deconstruction of the American republic for concentrated, centralized power—the exact opposite of the Founders' intentions. During the last century or so, America began the transformation into a kind of pseudo-constitutional or post-constitutional republic, in which the natural law truths of the Declaration of Independence and the justice and security of the Constitution are typically and repeatedly abused to, paradoxically, enshrine in law and justify as legitimate the progressive's autocratic and egalitarian agenda. This is not to say that every aspect of republicanism and constitutionalism has been uprooted or eclipsed. But manipulating and breaching the Constitution—by the courts, the elected branches, and the administrative state, and through the federal government's growing aggressiveness in controlling and coercing the individual—has become increasingly routine and commonplace. Moreover, such transgressions are mostly acquiesced to, or worse, celebrated by too many. And for those who take notice, there seem to be few remaining and effective avenues of recourse.

In his pamphlet (later book) *The Law* (1850), French economist and statesman Frédéric Bastiat (1801–1850) explained that the perversion of the law is the perversion of justice—justice being a primary purpose of the civil society. "[W]hen [the law] has exceeded its proper functions, it has not done so merely in some inconsequential and debatable matters. The law has gone further than this; it has acted in direct opposition to its own purpose. The law has been used to destroy its own objective: It has been applied to annihilating the justice that it was supposed to maintain; to limiting and destroying rights which its real purpose was to respect. The law has placed the collective force at the disposal of the unscrupulous who wish, without risk, to exploit the person, liberty, and property of others. It has converted plunder into a right, in order to protect plunder. And it has converted lawful defense into a crime, in order to punish lawful defense."[1]

As a consequence, and despite the democratic features of a republic, Tocqueville wrote in *Democracy in America* that the outcome is soft tyranny. Indeed, as if condemning modern progressives and the future administrative state, Tocqueville explained: "When the sovereign is elective, or narrowly watched by a legislature which is really elective and independent, the oppression that he exercises over individuals is sometimes greater, but it is always less degrading; because every man, when he is oppressed and disarmed, may still imagine that, while he yields obedience, it is to himself he yields it, and that it is to one of his own inclinations that all the rest give way. In like manner, I can understand that when the sovereign represents the nation and is dependent upon the people, the rights and the power of which every citizen is deprived serve not only the head of the state, but the state itself; and that private persons derive some return from the sacrifice of their independence which they have made to the public. To create a representation of the people in every centralized country is, therefore, to diminish the evil that extreme centralization may produce, but not get rid of it."[2]

Yes, not get rid of it, not completely. And from the seeds of this tyranny sprouts tyranny itself. Lest we forget: It is one thing for the individual to be all he can be, but it is quite another thing for the government to be all it can be. The former was born to be free; the latter was established with limits. Tocqueville observed that there is no end to the tinkering and bullying of a boundless government. Nothing is off-limits, not even the small events and details of life, leaving the spirit of democratic vibrancy and its popular allure gravely weakened. Tocqueville's warning bears repeating: "Subjection in minor affairs breaks out every day and is felt by the whole community indiscriminately. It does not drive men to resistance, but it crosses them at every turn, till they are led to surrender the exercise of their own will. Thus their spirit is gradually broken and their character enervated; whereas that obedience which is exacted on a few important but rare occasions only exhibits servitude at certain intervals and throws the burden of it upon a small number of men. It is in vain to summon a people who have been rendered so dependent on the central power to choose from time to time the representatives of that power; this rare and brief exercise of their free choice, however important it may be, will not prevent them from gradually losing the faculties of thinking, feeling, and acting for themselves, and thus gradually falling below the level of humanity."[3]

Once the individual's spirit is conquered in favor of proclaimed egalitarian ends, Tocqueville pointed out, "[t]he hatred that men bear to privilege increases in proportion as privileges become fewer and less considerable, so that democratic passions would seem to burn most fiercely just when they have least fuel. . . . When all conditions are unequal, no inequality is so great as to offend the eye, whereas the slightest dissimilarity is odious in the midst of general uniformity; the more complete this uniformity is, the more insupportable the sight of such a difference becomes. Hence it is natural that the love of equality should constantly increase together with the equality itself, and that it should grow by what it feeds on."[4] In other words, once the poison of jealousy, contempt, and even hatred enters the bloodstream of the body politic, a dark and foreboding bleakness will begin to cover the society, from which nothing good will come.

---

I confess that I often wonder what America will have become in fifty or one hundred years. What will the future hold for our children and grandchildren? Will they be free, happy, prosperous, independent, and secure? What will be left of our constitutional system? Will the Bill of Rights have the force of law? What about property rights? Will they matter? How many will remember or care to learn about our founding principles, as concisely and brilliantly set forth in the Declaration of Independence? How many remember or care today? What of the civil society—or the social compact? Will it have frayed beyond repair? Will we have been conquered from within, as Thomas Jefferson, Joseph Story, and Abraham Lincoln feared might be our fate? Will we have avoided the doom of Athens and Rome? If we are honest with ourselves, we must agree that the outcome is unclear. The reason: a century or so of progressive governance and schemes, targeting the uniqueness of America, including its founding principles and republican system.

Future generations will look back on what we have done and know the answers. They will draw their judgments about this generation and record them in their history books. What lessons will they have learned? What will they say about us?

Will they say that we were a wise and conscientious people who understood and appreciated the blessings of our existence and surroundings and prudentially and conscientiously cared for them; or will they say we were a self-indulgent and inattentive people, easily shepherded in one direction or another, who stole the future from our own children and generations yet born, and squandered an irreplaceable heritage?

I am frequently asked what can be done. I have attempted to provide some specific answers. In *Liberty and Tyranny*, I presented a manifesto of policies and actions that I believed would contribute to improving our society, if the political will for such plans could be mustered. Unfortunately, at this writing, despite Republican Party control of all the elected branches of the federal government and historic control of state legislatures and governorships, it seems most of the objectives will remain inert. In *The Liberty Amendments*, I argued for using Article V of the Constitution to bring together a convention of the states, the purpose of which is to bypass the federal Leviathan altogether and enable the states to consider constitutional avenues for restoring republican government. Indeed, I suggested eleven reform amendments that, if adopted, would go a long way toward returning the federal government to its intended place. While there has been a valorous grassroots effort, even many Republican state legislatures have rejected this vital constitutional plan. In *Plunder and Deceit*, I endeavored to highlight the extent to which the federal government is dragging and pushing the nation toward the abyss by focusing on the economic and financial calamity of unfettered spending and borrowing. Again, little amelioration of consequence appears either around the corner or in the offing.

Nonetheless, those of us whose eyes are open, whatever our numbers, have a moral obligation to try to rouse our fellow citizens to take a sober and critical look at the decaying societal conditions, from which truthful conclusions can be drawn and perhaps improvements made. I understand the daunting task, given the powerful tide against which we must swim and the condemnations and mockeries from those who fear such inquiries and wish to escape them. Yet there is neither virtue nor benefit in denial or self-censorship.

There is no possible escape from reality. And we can gain strength from our own history and the courage and wisdom of the Founding Fathers and so many others who came before us.

Besides, we have no choice.

# NOTES

## 1. Americanism

1. Mark R. Levin, *Liberty and Tyranny: A Conservative Manifesto* (New York: Threshold Editions, 2003), 193.
2. Thomas Jefferson, "Letter to Roger Weightman," June 24, 1826, Library of Congress, loc.gov/exhibits/Jefferson/214.html (March 1, 2017).
3. Declaration of Independence, https://www.archives.gov/founding-docs/declaration-transcript (March 1, 2017).
4. The Virginia Declaration of Rights, America's Founding Documents, National Archives, https://www.archives.gov/founding-docs/virginia-declaration-of-rights (March 1, 2017).
5. Constitution of Pennsylvania, A Declaration of the Rights of the Inhabitants of the Commonwealth or State of Pennsylvania, Avalon Project, Yale Law School, http://avalon.law.yale.edu/18th_century/pa08.asp (March 1, 2017).
6. Massachusetts Constitution of 1780, Part the First. A Declaration of the Rights of the Inhabitants of the Commonwealth of Massachusetts, http://press-pubs.uchicago.edu/Founders/print_documents/bill_of_rightss6.html (March 1, 2017).

7. Thomas Jefferson, "Letter to Henry Lee," May 8, 1825, Founders Online, National Archives, http://Founders.archives.gov/documents/Jefferson/98-01-02-5212 (March 1, 2017).
8. Bernard Bailyn, *The Ideological Origins of the American Revolution* (Cambridge, MA: Harvard University Press, 1992), 27.
9. John Locke, *The Second Treatise of Government* (New York: Barnes & Noble, 2004), ch. 2, sec. 6.
10. John Locke, *Essays on the Law of Nature*, ed. W. von Leyden (Oxford: Oxford University Press, 2007), 113.
11. Ibid., 115.
12. Ibid., 121.
13. Ibid., 113, quoting Aristotle, *Nicomachean Ethics*, trans. H. Rackham (Cambridge, MA: Harvard University Press, 1943), 20.
14. Shirley Robin Letwin, *On the History of the Idea of Law*, ed. Noel B. Reynolds (Cambridge: Cambridge University Press, 2008), 28, quoting Aristotle, *Rhetoric* I, 1373b, in *The Complete Works of Aristotle*, ed. Jonathan Barnes, vol. 2 (Princeton, NJ: Princeton University Press, 1984).
15. Marcus Tullius Cicero, *On the Republic*, *On the Laws*, I, xvi, ed. Jeffrey Henderson, trans. Clinton W. Keyes (Cambridge, MA: Harvard University Press, 2000), 345, 347; see ibid., I, x, xv, xvii.
16. Letwin, *On the History of the Idea of Law*, quoting Marcus Tullius Cicero, *De Republica*, III, xxii, ed. T. E. Page, trans. Clinton W. Keyes (Cambridge, MA: Harvard University Press, 1928), 33; Cicero, *On the Laws*, III, xxii, 211.
17. Algernon Sidney, *Discourses Concerning Government*, ed. Thomas West (Indianapolis, IN: Liberty Classics, 1990), v.
18. Ibid., 8, 32, 17.
19. Ibid., 192, 193.

20. John Locke, *Of Ethics in General*, in Peter King, *Life and Letters of John Locke* (London: George Bell & Sons, 1864), 311–12.
21. Alexander Hamilton, *The Farmer Refuted, &c*, Feb. 23, 1775, Founders Online, National Archives, http://Founders.archives.gov/documents/Hamilton/01-01-02-0057 (March 1, 2017).
22. Declaration of Independence.
23. Levin, *Liberty and Tyranny*, 26.
24. Ibid., 26–27.
25. Abraham Lincoln, "Speech at Lewistown, Illinois," August 17, 1858, *Chicago Press and Tribune*, August 21, 1858, in *Collected Works of Abraham Lincoln*, vol. 2 (Ann Arbor: University of Michigan Digital Library Production Services, 2001), 546–47, http://quod.lib.umich.edu/cgi/t/text/text-idx?c=lincoln;cc=lincoln;type=simple;rgn=div1;q1=Speech%20at%20Lewistown;view=text;subview=detail;sort=occur;idno=lincoln2;node=lincoln2%3A567 (March 3, 2017).
26. Murry N. Rothbard, *The Ethics of Liberty* (New York: New York University Press, 2002), 12, citing William Blackstone, *Commentaries on the Laws of England*, Book I, quoted in *The Natural Law Reader*, ed. Brendan F. Brown (New York: Oceana, 1960), 123.
27. Blackstone, *Commentaries*, Book I, 27.
28. Chester James Antieau, "Natural Rights and the Founding Fathers—The Virginians," 17 *Washington & Lee Law Review* 43, 55 (1960), http://scholarlycommons.law.wlu.edu/wlulr/vol17/iss1/4, quoting Thomas Jefferson, "Letter to Francis W. Gilmer," June 7, 1816; 10 Ford 32.
29. Ibid., quoting Thomas Jefferson, "Letter to Isaac H. Tiffany," April 4, 1819; Edward Dumbauld, *The Political Writings of Thomas Jefferson* (New York: Liberal Arts Press, 1955), 55.

30. Ibid., 52.
31. Peter James Stanlis, *Edmund Burke: The Enlightenment and Revolution* (Edison, NJ: Transaction, 1991), 213, citing Edmund Burke, "A Letter to a Noble Lord," *Works*, vol. 5 (Boston: Little, Brown, 1904), 186.
32. Ibid.
33. Declaration of Independence.
34. Ibid.

**2. The Progressive Masterminds**

1. Mark R. Levin, *Liberty and Tyranny: A Conservative Manifesto* (New York: Threshold Editions, 2009).
2. Mark R. Levin, *Ameritopia: The Unmaking of America* (New York: Threshold Editions, 2012).
3. Herbert Croly, *The Promise of American Life*, 1909, in *Classics of American Political & Constitutional Thought*, vol. 2, ed. Scott J. Hammond, Kevin R. Harwick, and Howard L. Lubert (Indianapolis, IN: Hackett, 2007), 297.
4. Ibid., 313.
5. Barack Obama, "Remarks by the President at a Campaign Event in Roanoke, Virginia," July 13, 2012, The White House, https://www.whitehouse.gov/the-press-office/2012/07/13/remarks-president-campaign-event-roanoke-virginia (March 2, 2017).
6. Croly, *The Promise of American Life*, 313.
7. Herbert D. Croly, *Progressive Democracy* (London: Forgotten Books, 2015), 29–30.
8. Ibid., 33.
9. Ibid., 39.
10. Ibid., 43, 44.
11. Ibid., 40.

12. Ibid.
13. Ibid., 376–77.
14. Herbert Croly, "The Eclipse of Progressivism," October 27, 1920, republished in the *New Republic*, December 31, 1969, https://newrepublic.com/article/73408/the-eclipse-progressivism (March 2, 2017).
15. Ibid.
16. Ibid.
17. Learned Hand, "Letter to Theodore Roosevelt," April 8, 1910, Learned Hand Papers, Harvard Law School, in *The New Deal and the Triumph of Liberalism*, ed. Sidney M. Milkus and Jerome M. Mileur (Amherst: University of Massachusetts Press, 2002), 65 n.19.
18. Theodore Roosevelt, "Nationalism and Popular Rule," *Outlook* 97 (January 21, 1911): 96.
19. Book Review, "The New Democracy," *The Independent* 72 (January–June 1912): 957, https://books.google.com/books?id=ljIPAQAAIAAJ (March 3, 2017).
20. Theodore Roosevelt, "Speech at Osawatomie, Kansas: The New Nationalism," August 31, 1910, http://www.theodore-roosevelt.com/images/research/speeches/trnationalismspeech.pdf (March 2, 2017).
21. Ibid.
22. Ibid.
23. Ibid.
24. Theodore Roosevelt, *The New Nationalism* (New York: Outlook, 1911), 37, 39.
25. Platform of the Progressive Party, August 7, 1912, Primary Sources, *American Experience*, PBS, http://www.pbs.org/wgbh/americanexperience/features/primary-resources/tr-progressive/ (March 2, 2017).

26. Woodrow Wilson, "Fourth of July Address on the Declaration of Independence," in *Classics of American Political & Constitutional Thought*, vol. 2, 318.
27. Ibid., 319.
28. Woodrow Wilson, *Constitutional Government in the United States* (New York: Columbia University Press, 1908), 16.
29. Ibid., 323.
30. Woodrow Wilson, "Address at Independence Hall: The Meaning of Liberty," July 4, 1914, American Presidency Project, http://www.presidency.ucsb.edu/ws/index.php?pid=65381 (March 2, 2017).
31. Calvin Coolidge, "Address at the Celebration of the 150th Anniversary of the Declaration of Independence, Philadelphia, PA," July 5, 1926, American Presidency Project, http://www.presidency.ucsb.edu/ws/?pid=408 (March 2, 2017).
32. Dick Lehr, "The Racist Legacy of Woodrow Wilson," November 25, 2015, *Atlantic*, https://www.theatlantic.com/politics/archive/2015/11/wilson-legacy-racism/417549/ (March 2, 2017); Eric S. Yellin, *Racism in the Nation's Service: Government Workers and the Color Line in Woodrow Wilson's America* (Chapel Hill: University of North Carolina Press, 2016).
33. Woodrow Wilson, *The New Freedom* ([N.p.]: Tutis Digital, 2008), 1.
34. Ibid., 7.
35. Ibid., 13.
36. Ibid., 89.
37. Ibid., 115.
38. Woodrow Wilson, *Study of Public Administration* (London: Forgotten Books, 2012), 4.
39. Ibid., 5.

40. Ibid., 7.
41. Ibid., 11–12.
42. Ibid., 13.
43. Ibid., 18–19.
44. Ibid., 16.
45. John Dewey, *Liberalism and Social Action* (Amherst, NY: Prometheus Books, 2000), 15, 16–17.
46. Ibid., 28.
47. John Dewey, "The Need for a New Party," March 31, 1931, *New Republic*, https://newrepublic.com/article/104638/the-need-new-party (March 2, 2017).
48. John Dewey, *Individualism Old and New* (Amherst, NY: Prometheus Books, 1999), 51.
49. Ibid., 58.
50. Ibid., 75–76.
51. Ibid., 77–78.
52. Ibid., 81–82.
53. John Dewey, "Address to the American Philosophical Association: The Future of Liberalism," December 28, 1934, First Principles Series, Heritage Foundation, http://origin.heritage.org/initiatives/first-principles/primary-sources/john-dewey-on-liberalisms-future (March 2, 2017).
54. Ibid.
55. Ibid.
56. John Dewey, *Democracy and Education* ([N.p.]: Simon & Brown, 2012), 86.
57. Ibid., 234.
58. Ibid., 239, 240, 245.
59. John Dewey, "What Are the Russian Schools Doing?" *New Re-*

*public*, December 5, 1928, https://newrepublic.com/article/92769/russia-soviet-education-communism (March 2, 2017).

60. Ibid.
61. Walter E. Weyl, *The New Democracy* (New York: Macmillan, 1912), 1, 4.
62. Ibid., 8–9.
63. Ibid., 12–13.
64. Ibid., 13.
65. Ibid., 15.
66. Alexis de Tocqueville, *Democracy in America* (New York: Knopf, 1994).
67. Ibid., vol. 1, 70.
68. Ibid., vol. 1, 71.
69. Ibid., vol. 1, 271
70. Ibid., vol. 1, 272.
71. Ibid., vol. 2, 102.
72. Ibid., vol. 2, 103–4.
73. Ibid., vol. 2, 318.
74. Ibid.
75. Ibid., vol. 2, 318–19.
76. Ibid., vol. 2, 319.
77. Ibid.
78. Ibid., vol. 2, 319–20.
79. Ibid., vol. 2, 321.

**3. The Philosopher-Kings**

1. Mark R. Levin, *Ameritopia: The Unmaking of America* (New York: Threshold Editions, 2012), xi.
2. Jean-Jacques Rousseau, *The Basic Writings*, *Discourse on the Origin*

of Inequality, 2nd ed., ed. and trans. Donald A. Cress (Indianapolis, IN: Hackett, 2012), 45.

3. Ibid.
4. John Locke, *The Second Treatise of Government* (New York: Barnes & Noble, 2004), ch. 2, sec. 6.
5. Rousseau, *Origin of Equality*, 67.
6. Ibid., 74–75.
7. Ibid., 87.
8. Rousseau, *Discourse on Political Economy*, 126.
9. Ibid., 132.
10. Ibid., 133.
11. Ibid.
12. Rousseau, *Discourse on Social Contract*, 192.
13. Ibid.
14. Ibid.
15. Ibid., 192–93.
16. Ibid., 222.
17. Ibid., 172.
18. G. W. F. Hegel, *Elements of the Philosophy of Right*, trans. S. W. Dyde (Mineola, NY: Dover, 2005), 132, 133.
19. Ibid., 133.
20. Ibid.
21. Ibid., 143.
22. Ibid.
23. Ibid., 162.
24. Karl R. Popper, *The Open Society and Its Enemies*, vol. 2 (Princeton, NJ: Princeton University Press, 1971), 40.
25. Hegel, *Philosophy of Right*, 155.
26. Ibid., 156.

27. Ibid.
28. Ibid., 157.
29. Ibid., 164, 165.
30. Popper, *The Open Society and Its Enemies*, 78–79.
31. Karl Marx, *The Communist Manifesto* (Lexington, KY: SoHo Books, 2010), 36.
32. Ibid., 19.
33. Ibid., 19, 20.
34. Ibid., 20, 21.
35. Ibid., 21.
36. Ibid., 23.
37. Ibid.
38. Raymond Aron, *The Opium of the Intellectuals* (New Brunswick, NJ: Transaction, 2007), 66.
39. Ibid., 70.
40. Ibid.
41. Ibid., 78.
42. Marx, *The Communist Manifesto*, 36.
43. Ibid., 38.
44. Ibid.
45. Ibid., 42.
46. Ibid.
47. Ibid., 42–43.
48. Popper, *The Open Society and Its Enemies*, 82, 83.
49. Ibid., 85.
50. Martin Malia, Foreword to *The Black Book of Communism: Crimes, Terror, Repression*, ed. Stéphane Courtois (Cambridge, MA: Harvard University Press, 1999), ix–xx.

**4. Administrative-State Tyranny**

1. Mark R. Levin, *Liberty and Tyranny: A Conservative Manifesto* (New York: Threshold Editions, 2009), 3–4.
2. James Madison, Alexander Hamilton, and John Jay, *The Federalist Papers*, No. 51, Avalon Project, http://avalon.law.yale.edu/18th_century/fed51.asp (March 2, 2017).
3. Declaration of Independence, https://www.archives.gov/founding-docs/declaration-transcript (March 1, 2017).
4. F. A. Hayek, *The Fatal Conceit: The Errors of Socialism*, ed. W. W. Bartley III (Chicago: University of Chicago Press, 1988), 55.
5. Ibid., 53, 54.
6. Friedrich Hayek, *The Constitution of Liberty* (Chicago: University of Chicago Press, 1978), 82.
7. Mark R. Levin, *Plunder and Deceit: Big Government's Exploitation of Young People and the Future* (New York: Threshold Editions, 2015).
8. Ibid., 37–51 ("On Social Security"); 53–71 ("On Medicare and Obamacare").
9. Levin, *Liberty and Tyranny*, 68.
10. Levin, *Plunder and Deceit*, 53–71 ("On Medicare and Obamacare").
11. Ibid., 73–90 ("On Education").
12. Ibid., 23–36 ("On Debt").
13. Ibid., 117–18.

**5. Liberty and Republicanism**

1. Thomas Jefferson, "Letter to Isaac H. Tiffany," April 4, 1819, Founders Online, National Archives, https://Founders.archives.gov/documents/Jefferson/98-01-02-0303 (March 3, 2017).
2. John Stuart Mill, *On Liberty*, ed. Charles W. Elliot (New York: Barnes & Noble, 2004), 79, 80.

3. Ibid., 80.
4. Ibid., 80–81.
5. John Stuart Mill, "Utilitarianism," ch. 2, (1863), Utilitarianism Resources, https://www.utilitarianism.com/mill2.htm (March 3, 2017).
6. John Stuart Mill, "Utilitarianism," ch. 4, (1863), Utilitarianism Resources, https://www.utilitarianism.com/mill4.htm (March 3, 2017).
7. Thomas Jefferson, "Letter to John Adams," December 10, 1819, Founders Online, National Archives, https://Founders.archives.gov/?q=freedom%20%20virtue%20Author%3A%22Jefferson%2C%20Thomas%22&s=1211311111&sa=&r=8&sr (March 3, 2017).
8. Charles Montesquieu, *The Spirit of the Laws*, ed. Anne M. Cohler, Basia C. Miller, and Harold S. Stone (Cambridge: Cambridge University Press, 2009), Part 1, Book 3, Chapter 3.
9. Ibid., 1:3:8.
10. Ibid., 1:3:3.
11. John Adams, "Novanglus, Thoughts on Government," in *The Works of John Adams*, vol. 4, ed. Charles Frances Adams (1851), Online Library of Liberty, http://oll.libertyfund.org/titles/adams-the-works-of-john-adams-vol-4 (March 3, 2017).
12. Virginia Declaration of Rights, *America's Founding Documents*, National Archives, https://www.archives.gov/founding-docs/virginia-declaration-of-rights (March 1, 2017).
13. Constitution of Pennsylvania, A Declaration of the Rights of the Inhabitants of the Commonwealth or State of Pennsylvania, Avalon Project, Yale Law School, http://avalon.law.yale.edu/18th_century/pa08.asp (March 1, 2017).
14. Massachusetts Constitution of 1780, Part the First. A Declaration

of the Rights of the Inhabitants of the Commonwealth of Massachusetts, http://press-pubs.uchicago.edu/Founders/print_documents/bill_of_rightss6.html (March 1, 2017).

15. Russell Kirk, *The Conservative Mind* (Washington, DC: Regnery, 1986), 100.
16. Mill, *On Liberty*, 14.
17. Ibid., 14–15.
18. Isaiah Berlin, "Two Concepts of Liberty," in *Four Essays on Liberty* (Oxford: Oxford University Press, 1969), https://www.wiso.uni-hamburg.de/fileadmin/wiso_vwl/johannes/Ankuendigungen/Berlin_twoconceptsofliberty.pdf (March 3, 2017).
19. Ibid.
20. "Positive and Negative Liberty," *Stanford Encyclopedia of Philosophy*, February 27, 2003, revised August 2, 2016, https://plato.stanford.edu/entries/liberty-positive-negative/#Bib (March 3, 2017).
21. Ibid.
22. Ibid.
23. Berlin, "Two Concepts of Liberty," 1.
24. Ibid.
25. Ibid., 3.
26. Ibid., 4, 5.
27. Ibid., 7, 8.
28. Ibid., 9.
29. Ibid.
30. Ibid., 10.
31. Philip Pettit, *Republicanism: A Theory of Freedom and Government* (Oxford: Oxford University Press, 2010), 30.
32. U.S. Constitution, https://www.archives.gov/founding-docs/constitution (March 3, 2017).
33. Pettit, *Republicanism*, 30.

34. Ibid., 31.
35. Ibid., 35.
36. Ibid., 36.
37. Ibid., 36–37.
38. Bill of Rights, Founders Online, National Archives, https://www.archives.gov/founding-docs/bill-of-rights (March 3, 2017).
39. Berlin, "Two Concepts of Liberty," 2.
40. Ibid., 11.
41. Ibid., 13.
42. Auguste Comte, *A General View of Positivism* (London: Forgotten Books, 2015), 1.
43. John Stuart Mill, *Auguste Comte and Positivism* (New York: Cosimo Classics, 2008), 12, 13.
44. Comte, *A General View of Positivism*, 8, 9.
45. Ibid., 236, 237.
46. Bernard Bailyn, *The Ideological Origins of the American Revolution* (Cambridge, MA: Belknap Press of Harvard University Press, 1992), 55, 57–59.
47. Montesquieu, *The Spirit of the Laws*, 1:3:10.
48. Ibid., 1:5:14.
49. Ibid., 1:8:2.
50. Ibid., 2:2:6.
51. U.S. Constitution.
52. James Madison, Alexander Hamilton, and John Jay, *The Federalist Papers*, No. 47, Avalon Project, Yale Law School, http://avalon.law.yale.edu/18th_century/fed47.asp (March 2, 2017).
53. Ibid., No. 51, http://avalon.law.yale.edu/18th_century/fed51.asp (March 2, 2017).
54. Johannes Althusius, *Politica: An Abridged Translation of Politics Methodically Set Forth and Illustrated with Sacred and Profane Ex-*

*amples*, ed. Frederick S. Carney (Indianapolis, IN: Liberty Fund, 1995), 62.

55. Ibid., 191.
56. Alison L. LaCroix, *The Ideological Origins of American Federalism* (Cambridge, MA: Harvard University Press, 2010), 132–33.
57. James Madison, Alexander Hamilton, and John Jay, *The Federalist Papers*, No. 9, Avalon Project, Yale Law School, http://avalon.law.yale.edu/18th_century/fed09.asp (March 2, 2017).
58. Ibid., No. 32, http://avalon.law.yale.edu/18th_century/fed32.asp (March 2, 2017).
59. Ibid., No. 39, http://avalon.law.yale.edu/18th_century/fed39.asp (March 2, 2017).
60. Ibid., No. 45, http://avalon.law.yale.edu/18th_century/fed45.asp (March 2, 2017).
61. U.S. Constitution.
62. Russell Kirk, *The Roots of American Order* (Wilmington, DE: Intercollegiate Studies Institute, 2003), 416.
63. Woodrow Wilson, *Constitutional Government in the United States* (New York: Columbia University Press, 1911), 54.
64. Ibid., 56, 57.
65. Ibid., 70.
66. Bruce P. Frohnen and George W. Carey, *Constitutional Morality and the Rise of Quasi-Law* (Cambridge, MA: Harvard University Press, 2016), 218.
67. Maeve P. Carey, "Counting Regulations: An Overview of Rulemaking, Types of Federal Regulations, and Pages in the *Federal Register*," October 4, 2016, Congressional Research Service, https://fas.org/sgp/crs/misc/R43056.pdf (March 3, 2017).
68. Clyde Wayne Crews, "The 2017 Unconstitutionality Index: 18 Federal Rules for Every Law Congress Passes," *OpenMarket*,

Competitive Enterprise Institute, https://cei.org/blog/2017-unconstitutionality-index-18-federal-rules-every-law-congress-passes (March 3, 2017).

69. Montesquieu, *The Spirit of the Laws*, 1:1:3.
70. Ibid., 3:19:3.
71. Ibid., 3:19:5.
72. Adam Smith, *The Theory of Moral Sentiments*, ed. Ryan Patrick Hanley (New York: Penguin Books, 2009), 275–76.

**6. Liberty and Property**

1. Mark R. Levin, *Liberty and Tyranny: A Conservative Manifesto* (New York: Threshold Editions, 2009), 62.
2. John Locke, *The Second Treatise of Government*, ed. Peter Laslett (Cambridge: Cambridge University Press, 2003), sec. 138, 360.
3. William Blackstone, *Commentaries on the Laws of England*, 3rd ed., ed. Thomas M. Cooley, vol. 1 (Chicago: Callaghan, 1884), 138.
4. John Adams, "Defence of the Constitutions of Government of the United States," Founders' Constitution, http://press-pubs.uchicago.edu/Founders/documents/v1ch15s34.html (March 3, 2017).
5. James Madison, "Property," March 29, 1792, Founders' Constitution, http://press-pubs.uchicago.edu/Founders/documents/v1ch16s23.html (March 3, 2017).
6. F. A. Hayek, *Individualism and Economic Order* (Chicago: University of Chicago Press, 1980), 10–11.
7. Ibid., 14.
8. Ibid., 15–16.
9. Ibid., 22.

10. Ibid., 29.
11. Ibid., 24–25.
12. F. A. Hayek, *The Road to Serfdom* (Chicago: University of Chicago Press, 1994), 41.
13. Ibid., 44–45.
14. "Address of the Annapolis Convention," September 14, 1786, Founders Online, National Archives, https://Founders.archives.gov/documents/Hamilton/01-03-02-0556 (March 3, 2017).
15. Joseph Story, *A Familiar Exposition of the Constitution of the United States* (Washington, DC: Regnery Gateway, 1986), sec. 163, 139–40.
16. U.S. Constitution, https://www.archives.gov/founding-docs/constitution (March 3, 2017).
17. Raoul Berger, "Judicial Manipulation of the Commerce Clause," 74 *Texas Law Review* 695, 704–705 (March 1996) (internal citations omitted).
18. Barry Friedman and Genevieve Lakier, "'To Regulate' Not 'To Prohibit': Limiting the Commerce Power," April 3, 2013, *Supreme Court Review* 2012, NYU School of Law, Public Law, and Legal Theory, research paper No. 13-13; NYU School of Law, Law and Economics, Research Paper No. 13-10, https://www.heartland.org/_template-assets/documents/publications/ssrn-id2244496.pdf (March 4, 2017), 265.
19. Milton Friedman, *Capitalism and Freedom* (Chicago: University of Chicago Press, 2002), 8, 9–10.
20. Ibid., 23, 24.
21. Ibid., 196–97.
22. Ibid., 197.
23. Levin, *Liberty and Tyranny*, 7–8.

24. Mark R. Levin, *Plunder and Deceit: Big Government's Exploitation of Young People and the Future* (New York: Threshold Editions, 2015), 31.
25. Jim Powell, *FDR's Folly: How Roosevelt and His New Deal Prolonged the Great Depression* (New York: Three Rivers Press, 2003); Amity Shlaes, *The Forgotten Man: A New History of the Great Depression* (New York: Harper, 2007).
26. Harold L. Cole and Lee E. Ohanian, "How Government Prolonged the Depression," *Wall Street Journal*, February 2, 2009, https://www.wsj.com/articles/SB123353276749137485 (March 3, 2017).
27. Friedman, *Capitalism and Freedom*, 38.
28. Ibid., 45.
29. Ibid., 50.
30. Robert E. Lucas, Jr., *Lectures on Economic Growth* (Cambridge, MA: Harvard University Press, 2004), 109.
31. James R. Otteson, "An Audacious Promise: The Moral Case for Capitalism," *Issues 2012*, No. 12, Manhattan Institute for Public Research (May 2012).
32. Levin, *Liberty and Tyranny*, 61.
33. George Reisman, *Capitalism* (Ottawa, IL: Jameson Books, 1996), 76–77.
34. Lucas, *Lectures*, 169.
35. Hernando de Soto, *The Mystery of Capital: Why Capitalism Triumphs in the West and Fails Everywhere Else* (New York: Basic Books, 2000), 6–7.
36. Ibid., 7–8.
37. Charles Montesquieu, *The Spirit of the Laws*, ed. Anne M. Cohler, Basia C. Miller, and Harold S. Stone (Cambridge: Cambridge University Press, 2009), Part 1, Book 5, Chapter 6.
38. Ibid., 4:20:1.

39. Ibid., 4:20:4.
40. Ibid., 4:20:3.
41. Ibid., 3:18:7.
42. Ibid., 4:20:4.
43. Karl Popper, *The Poverty of Historicism* (London: Routledge Classics, 2010), 64.

**Epilogue**

1. Frederic Bastiat, *The Law* (Mansfield Centre, CT: Martino, 2011), 6.
2. Alexis de Tocqueville, *Democracy in America*, vol. 2 (New York: Penguin Classics, 2003), 320.
3. Ibid., 320–21.
4. Ibid., 295.